Kawaii DOODLES

Supercute Drawings in Four Easy Steps!

yuu

TUTTLE Publishing

Tokyo | Rutland, Vermont | Singapore

Contents

1 Cute Kawaii Characters

Let's Draw People (Faces)

Let's Draw People (Bodies)

Let's Draw Animals

Let's Draw Insects

Let's Draw Sea Creatures

Let's Draw Kawaii Characters

Let's Draw Animal Characters

2 Cute Kawaii Items

Let's Draw Clothes

Let's Draw Stylish Items

Let's Draw Favorite Furnishings

5 Give the Gift of Kawaii

· ·

Why I Wrote This Book

Have you ever thought that you'd like to improve your drawing, but you don't know how to go about it? Do you admire Kawaii style but you're not sure how to draw these addictively cute pictures? Then you've come to the right place! I created this guide for everyone who loves drawing and the simple iconic sweetness of Kawaii! Simply follow the four steps (sometimes five!) and copy the cute Kawaii icons. Personalizing messages and presents for your family and friends are a perfect way to show off your newfound Kawaii cool! So get some pens and paper ready and let your Kawaii doodle journey begin!

—YUU

Recommended Pens

Here we take a look at the kinds of pens it's good to have on hand. But whatever pens you have or prefer are fine for doodling and creating cute Kawaii illustrations!

Great for drawing lines and coloring in!

The pen that plays the leading role: this one gets used the most

Water-based pen

Dark-colored pens are ideal for drawing illustrations. I recommend a pen about 0.5mm thick that creates a strong, clear line.

Colored ballpoint pen

Colored pens are great for creating lines or filling in color. Adding even a little color instantly gives illustrations a cute Kawaii touch!

Use these to color in larger areas!

Great for writing on photographs

Pen for writing on photos

These pens create a neat, distinct line when drawing on photos. It's good to have one on hand.

Colored pencils

These are recommended for coloring in large areas. They add soft highlights, and you're unlikely to make mistakes.

How to Use This Book

❶ ❷ ❸ ⋯ Follow the steps and copy the drawings. Soon you'll be able to create these cute Kawaii doodles easily!

★ ❶,❷,❸ ⋯ Practice by following the steps in the right order.
★ Once you've drawn the picture, refer to the sample to color it in.
★ For those who want to draw more, try creating variations.

Name of illustration

Completion
The last step is the finished drawing.

Tips
Here, I offer suggestions, tricks and things to watch out for.

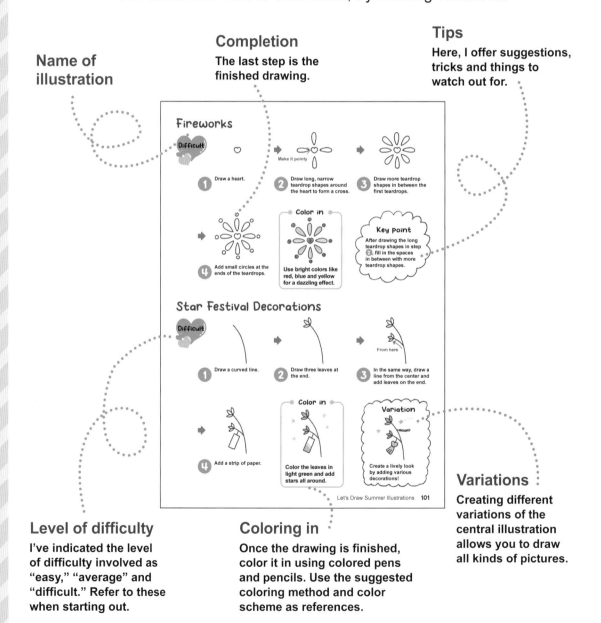

Level of difficulty
I've indicated the level of difficulty involved as "easy," "average" and "difficult." Refer to these when starting out.

Coloring in
Once the drawing is finished, color it in using colored pens and pencils. Use the suggested coloring method and color scheme as references.

Variations
Creating different variations of the central illustration allows you to draw all kinds of pictures.

1

Cute Kawaii Characters

Let's start by drawing pictures of people and animals. Try drawing hairstyles and fashions similar to your own, or reimagine yourself as an animal. Have fun creating an alter ego in cure Kawaii form!

Let's Draw People  Faces

You'll want to start by drawing your own face in a cute way, right? Once you can draw yourself, try drawing the faces of your loved ones, such as family and friends.

Have fun changing hairstyles and expressions to create lots of different versions.

Basic Girl

Easy

From here

1 Draw a wide circle and add small ears on each side.

2 Draw wavy bangs and draw in a ponytail on the top of the head.

3 Just below the center of the face, draw a pointy mountain for the nose.

4 Draw in round eyes on either side of the nose.

5 Draw a U below the nose to make the mouth.

● Color in ●

Adding a bow and coloring in the cheeks will make it cute.

Older Sister

 Average

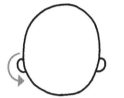

1 Draw a long, rounded face and add small ears on each side.

2 Draw in a side part on the right and add a small ponytail.

3 Make a small < shape just below the center of the face for the nose.

4 Draw in round eyes on either side of the nose and add one eyelash on the upper left of each eye.

5 Draw in a relaxed curve beneath the nose to make the mouth.

Color in

For the hair, add in only brown lines for a stylish look.

Girl with Big Eyes

Difficult

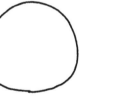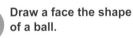

1 Draw a face the shape of a ball.

2 Draw in diagonal bangs and join vertical lines to the chin on both sides for the rest of the hair.

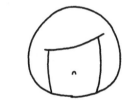

3 Draw a small mountain just below the center of the face for the nose.

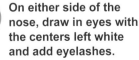

4 On either side of the nose, draw in eyes with the centers left white and add eyelashes.

5 Draw in a V-shaped mouth.

Color in

Coloring the cheeks pink makes it even cuter!

Boy

Easy

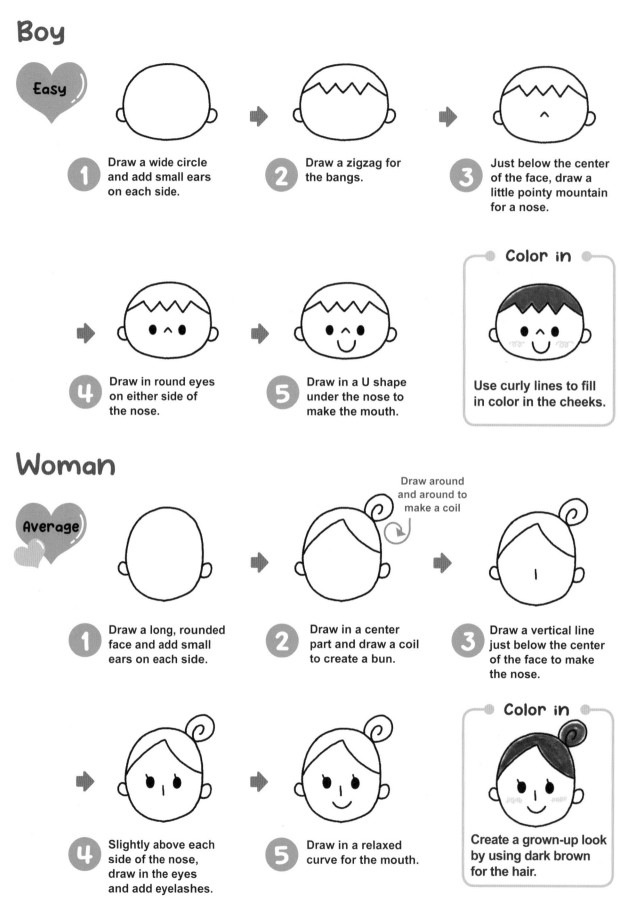

1 Draw a wide circle and add small ears on each side.

2 Draw a zigzag for the bangs.

3 Just below the center of the face, draw a little pointy mountain for a nose.

4 Draw in round eyes on either side of the nose.

5 Draw in a U shape under the nose to make the mouth.

Color in

Use curly lines to fill in color in the cheeks.

Woman

Average

1 Draw a long, rounded face and add small ears on each side.

2 Draw in a center part and draw a coil to create a bun.

Draw around and around to make a coil

3 Draw a vertical line just below the center of the face to make the nose.

4 Slightly above each side of the nose, draw in the eyes and add eyelashes.

5 Draw in a relaxed curve for the mouth.

Color in

Create a grown-up look by using dark brown for the hair.

Man

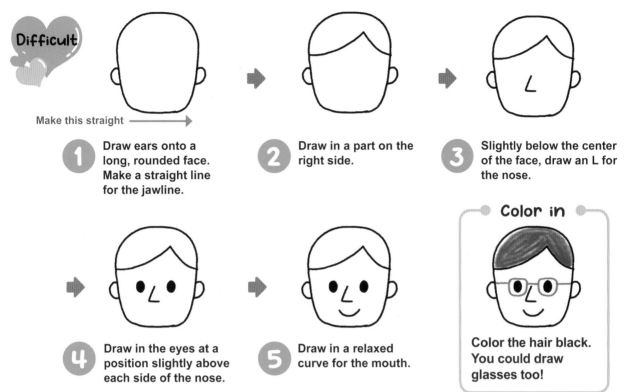

Difficult

Make this straight ⟶

1 Draw ears onto a long, rounded face. Make a straight line for the jawline.

2 Draw in a part on the right side.

3 Slightly below the center of the face, draw an L for the nose.

4 Draw in the eyes at a position slightly above each side of the nose.

5 Draw in a relaxed curve for the mouth.

Color in

Color the hair black. You could draw glasses too!

You Can Draw Older People Too

Let's add wrinkles and change the hair color.

woman

Older woman

Add wrinkles by drawing in 八 shaped lines on either side of the mouth. For the hair, use gray and create a bun below the ear.

man

Older man

Draw wrinkles and hair as for the older woman. Small glasses are best.

Let's Change the Hairstyle

Braids

Easy

1. Draw a wide circle and add ears and lines of hair for the bangs.

2. Draw in the eyes, nose and mouth.

3. Draw three circles beneath the ears to make braids.

Color in

Create a zigzag finish at the ends of the hair for a natural look.

Variation

Drawing wavy lines below the ears transforms the hairstyle into a relaxed perm worn loose!

Topknot

Average

1. Draw a wide circle and add ears. Draw three lines on the face above the ears.

2. Draw in the eyes, nose and mouth.

3. Make a fluffy shape on top of the head.

Make a fluffy look

Color in

Use messy circles to fill in the color on the bun.

Variation

Placing the bun below the ear creates a laid-back look.

Long Hair

Average

Join to the opposite side

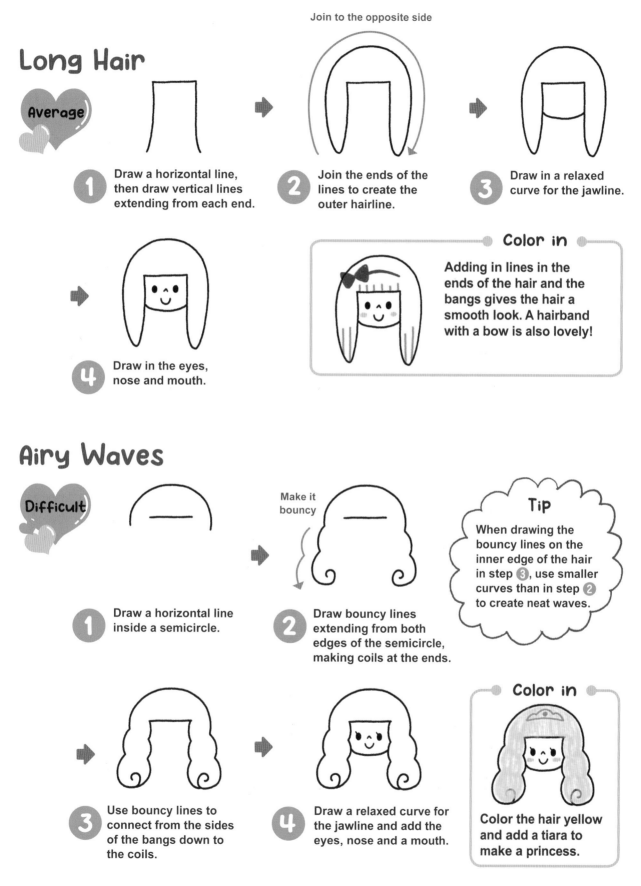

1 Draw a horizontal line, then draw vertical lines extending from each end.

2 Join the ends of the lines to create the outer hairline.

3 Draw in a relaxed curve for the jawline.

4 Draw in the eyes, nose and mouth.

● Color in ●

Adding in lines in the ends of the hair and the bangs gives the hair a smooth look. A hairband with a bow is also lovely!

Airy Waves

Difficult

Make it bouncy

1 Draw a horizontal line inside a semicircle.

2 Draw bouncy lines extending from both edges of the semicircle, making coils at the ends.

Tip

When drawing the bouncy lines on the inner edge of the hair in step **3**, use smaller curves than in step **2** to create neat waves.

3 Use bouncy lines to connect from the sides of the bangs down to the coils.

4 Draw a relaxed curve for the jawline and add the eyes, nose and a mouth.

● Color in ●

Color the hair yellow and add a tiara to make a princess.

Let's Draw Different Expressions

Smiling

 Easy

1 Draw the face and hair in step **2** from page 10.

2 Draw in a small pointy mountain below the center of the face for the nose.

3 Draw in mountain shapes on either sides of the nose for the eyes.

4 Draw in a U shape below the nose to make the mouth.

Color in

Use three short parallel lines for the cheeks.

Variation

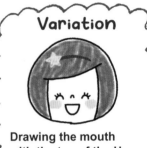

Drawing the mouth with the top of the U closed creates the look of a big, happy smile.

Excited!

Easy

1 Draw the face and hair in step **2** from page 10.

2 Draw in a small pointy mountain below the center of the face for the nose.

3 Draw in arrow-like shapes for the eyes.

4 Draw a lidded U shape for the mouth.

Color in

For the cheeks, leave in jagged lines on purpose.

Variation

Using an arrow shape for only one eye creates a winking look.☆

Angry!

Average

1 Draw the face and hair in step **2** from page 10.

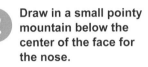

2 Draw in a small pointy mountain below the center of the face for the nose.

3 Draw short diagonal lines on either side of the nose to make slanted eyes.

4 Draw a mountain beneath the nose to make the mouth.

Color in

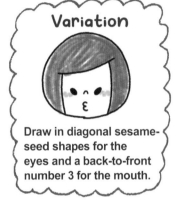

Make the cheeks red to convey anger.

Variation

Draw in diagonal sesame-seed shapes for the eyes and a back-to-front number 3 for the mouth.

Disappointed

Average

1 Draw the face and hair in step **2** from page 10.

2 Draw in a small pointy mountain below the center of the face for the nose.

3 Draw in short diagonal lines on either side of the nose for drooping eyes.

4 Draw in a wavy line beneath the nose to make the mouth.

Color in

As this face isn't cheerful, keep the cheek color minimal.

Variation

Make the mouth a ⌒ shape. This creates the look of regretting having made a mistake.

Various Expressions

The eyes and nose stay the same. Add eyebrows and other features.

Draw up to step ❹ on page 10.

Broad smile
The look of having had a good idea. Draw vertical lines inside the crescent moon-shaped mouth.

Anticipating something delicious
Make a rounded loop at the edge of the U-shaped mouth. Add horizontal lines at the top of the eyes too.

Cheerful
Drawing a back-to-front number 3 for the mouth makes for a whistling expression.

Add ellipses over the head

Awkward
To express an awkward situation, draw a bead of sweat on the forehead and a straight line for the mouth.

Sobbing
Downward-pointing eyebrows and a teardrop are the key points. Add droplets above the head.

Add a curly line at the top of the head.

Adding circles over the head makes for a drowsy look.

Anxious
Draw vertical lines beside the eyes and wavy lines around the head.

Annoyed
Make the eyebrows a crooked loop and finish the face with a ⌒ shape for the mouth.

Sleepy
Adding horizontal lines through the eyes creates a sleepy look.

If you change the eyes and mouth, you can make all kinds of expressions.

Draw up to step ❸ on page 10.

Color "heart eyes" in pink for the best result.

In love
Use hearts for eyes to show a young girl in love. The mouth is an inverted triangle.

Gentle smile
Use U shapes for the eyes and mouth to create a soft smile.

"Delicious"
Add a line at the side of the mouth to express munching.

"Yay!"
Use a mountain shape for one eye and draw a U-shaped mouth with the tongue slightly sticking out.

"So busy!"
Make coil shapes for the eyes to indicate a whirlwind-type busyness.

The trick is to draw the mouth low on the face!

Adding vertical lines at the side of the eyes makes for an even more shocked look.

"Oh no!"
Draw crosses for the eyes and make a long circle for the mouth.

Surprised
Use small dots surrounded by circles to express the eyes open wide in surprise.

Shocked
The shock has caused the eyes to roll back in the head, exposing the whites! Use a square for the mouth.

Let's Draw People  Bodies

Once you can draw faces, it's time for a lesson on bodies! Have fun moving arms and legs into various poses and playing dress-up.

The usual way to draw is to start with the face, then the body and then add the limbs.

Basic Girl

Average

1 Draw the face from page 10.

2 For clothes, draw a triangle beneath the face.

Make rounded

3 Add arms on both sides of the clothes. Make the hands rounded.

4 Draw legs beneath the clothing.

Color in

Color in the clothes. You can add patterns too!

Tip
When drawing clothing in step **2**, changing the size of the triangle allows you to alter the style of the dress.

Woman

Average

1 Draw the face of the woman on page 12.

2 Draw a long triangle beneath the face as clothing.

Make it long

3 Add arms on both sides of the dress. Make the hands rounded.

4 Draw legs beneath the clothing. Make the toes pointed so the feet face outward.

5 Draw horizontal lines at the wrists and ankles. Make a line of three little circles on the chest.

Color in

Color down to the ankles black to make leggings.

Draw a square silhouette.

Draw the boy's face from page 12

Draw the man's face from page 13

Make the width of the square body about the same as that of the face.

Add triangle sleeves to a square body.

For the shorts, think of joining two squares together.

For the pants, join two rectangles together.

Boy

Man

Various Poses

Greeting

Easy

1 Use the girl's face on page 10 as a reference to draw the face.

2 Draw a triangle for a dress beneath the face.

3 In the center of the dress, draw both hands together.

4 Draw the legs beneath the clothing. Point the toes to make them face slightly inward.

Color in

Color in the dress, avoiding the arms.

Hello!

Variation

Make one arm waving "bye." Try drawing the hand as if it's wearing a glove.

Seated

Average

1 Using page 10 as a reference, draw the face.

2 Draw a triangle beneath the face for the clothes, leaving the center slightly open.

Leave the center open

3 Draw the arms to follow the lines of the dress. Make the tips of the fingers slightly pointed so they turn outwards.

4 Draw in legs which taper to a point in the open space at the base of the dress.

Color in

Just taking a break

Draw in lines on either sides of the dress hem to create the look of a chair.

Variation

Drawing the hands together at the front of the dress and showing just a little of the knees creates the appearance of kneeling.

Walking

Average

1. Using page 10 as a reference, draw the face.

2. Draw a triangle for a dress beneath the face.

3. Add arms on either side of the dress. Make the hands rounded.

Make the points face in the same direction

4. Now add the legs and feet.

Color in

Add three strokes next to the foot to indicate walking

step...
step ...

Variation

Bend the arm and the leg at the back to create a running pose.

Jumping

Average

1. Using page 10 as a reference, draw the face.

2. Draw a triangle for a dress beneath the face.

3. Draw the arms on both sides of the dress. Make the elbows bent and the hands rounded.

Bend the arms

4. Draw the legs beneath the dress, with the legs out to the sides in line with the hem.

Color in

Add a cloud-shaped speech bubble near the feet.

Yay!

Variation

Opening the arms and legs out wide in a star shape creates a dynamic look.

Let's Play Dress-Up

Winter Coat

 Average

1 Use page 15 as a reference and draw the face.

2 Draw the sleeves beneath the face.

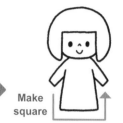 Make square

3 Create a square to join the underarms together and form a coat.

4 Add rounded hands at the ends of the sleeves and draw lines for the legs beneath the coat.

5 Draw the boots. Add the collar at the neckline and draw a line of buttons beneath it.

Color in

Add blue lines on the legs to make striped tights!

Uniform

 Average

1 Use page 14 as a reference to draw the face.

 Make them short

2 Draw sleeves beneath the face.

3 Join the underarms by drawing a square and add a trapezoid beneath it for the skirt.

4 Draw the arms at the ends of the sleeves and the legs beneath the skirt.

5 Add the collar and bow at the neck. Draw lines for the socks and shoes on the legs.

Color in

Make a check pattern for the skirt.

T-Shirt and Jeans

Average

1. Draw the older sister face from page 11.

This is the sleeve

2. Draw an arrow shape beneath the face to form the T-shirt.

3. Draw long rectangles beneath the T-shirt to make jeans.

4. Draw the arms at the ends of the sleeves and add feet at the hems of the jeans.

5. Add lines to make a V-shaped collar in the top and rolled-up hems in the jeans.

Color in

Making the hems a different color works well.

Princess Dress

Difficult

1. Draw the airy waves face from page 15.

2. Draw a collar with scalloped edging beneath the face and add puffed sleeves.

3. Draw in the line of the body to connect from underarm to underarm.

Make a full, airy triangle

4. Draw a full, airy triangle shape for the skirt.

5. Draw the arms at the ends of the sleeves and add lines for gloves.

Color in

Use two colors for the dress for a luxurious look!

Little Extras for Easy Costume Changes

Use the triangle dress as a base to add decoration and accessories!

Add a beret on top of the head and fill it in with color.

Start by drawing the girl from page 20.

Lovely dress
The heart-shaped pockets on this dress are very sweet. The square, open neckline gives it a casual look.

Stylish dress
A stylish dress with a rounded collar. Use a line to make the pochette bag hang over one shoulder in a cross-body style.

Make scalloped lines for the lace on the chest.

Color in above the knees to make leggings.

Jumper
If you draw in lines for the sleeves, you'll create the look of a T-shirt. Add a line in the center of the hem.

Grown-up dress for winter
Draw a heart-shaped bag for the girl to carry. Coloring the boots brown makes for a mature look.

Striped summer dress
Add blue to the striped pattern. Adding a check-like pattern to the bag creates the look of a basket.

Changing the shape of the clothes makes for more and more fashion choices!

Refer to the girl on page 20.

Favorite underwear
For the pants, use scalloped lines for the hems and create an airy look.

Red carpet dress
The key is to make the dress flare out from the waist. Use a lot of scalloped lines for an extravagant look.

Using a scribble pattern to add color increases the fluffy look.

Add a woolly edge to the coat hem.

Casual wear
Denim pants are perfect for having some serious fun. Adding lines at the waist and hems makes for an authentic denim look.

Sweater dress
A garment that tapers in slightly at the hem. To indicate the knit stitches, draw lines of ().

Warm coat
The cape and gloves look warm, don't they? To make the ice skates, add lines beneath the boots.

Let's Draw Animals!

There are so many cute animals to doodle and Kawaii-ify! You can create an entire zoo just for you!

Be aware of the animals' different characteristics, such as the shape of the ears and tail, when creating your cute characters.

Rabbit

Easy

Make the top rounded

1. Draw a wide circle and add long ears on top of the head.

2. Add eyes, nose and mouth in the lower part of the face. Use a line to join the nose and mouth.

3. Draw a small urn shape beneath the face to make the body.

4. Draw a W shape on the body to make the legs and add the round tail at the side.

Color in

Color the insides of the ears and the cheeks pink. A bow also looks cute.

Variation

For a gray rabbit, color everything except the area around the mouth.

Cat

Easy

Draw short lines

1 Draw a wide round face and add triangles on top of the head for ears.

2 Draw eyes, nose, mouth and whiskers on the lower part of the face.

3 Draw a small urn shape beneath the face for the body.

4 Draw a W shape on the front of the body for the legs and add a long tail at the side.

Color in

I used brown for the markings and pink for the nose.

Variation

Add brown lines on the face and body to make tabby markings.

Panda

Average

1 Draw a wide, round face and draw round ears on top of the head.

2 Draw long circles in the lower part of the face.

3 Add eyes inside the long circles and draw the nose and mouth.

Round the corners

4 Make a rounded square beneath the face for the body.

5 Add arms and legs on both sides of the body and color in.

Color in

Color the markings pink for a cute look.

Bear

Average

1 Draw a wide, round face and add round ears on top of the head.

2 Add the eyes, nose and mouth in the lower part of the face.

3 Use one line to draw the body and four legs together. Add a round tail to the backside.

Visualize joining squares together

Color in

Add color, leaving the inside of the ears and the area around the nose and mouth white.

Variations

Add brown lines to the face and body to transform the bear into a tiger!

Color around the eyes and add stripes to the tail to create a racoon dog (tanuki)!

Dog

Average

1 Draw a wide, round face.

2 Draw seed-like ears over the outline for the head and color them in.

3 Draw the eyes, nose and mouth in the lower part of the face. Use a line to connect the nose and mouth.

Make them uneven

4 Use one line to draw the body and legs together. Add the tail on the backside and draw a line around the neck.

Color in

Add markings on the back and color the collar.

Variation

Make the ears and tail fluffy for a cute toy-sized dog.

Pig

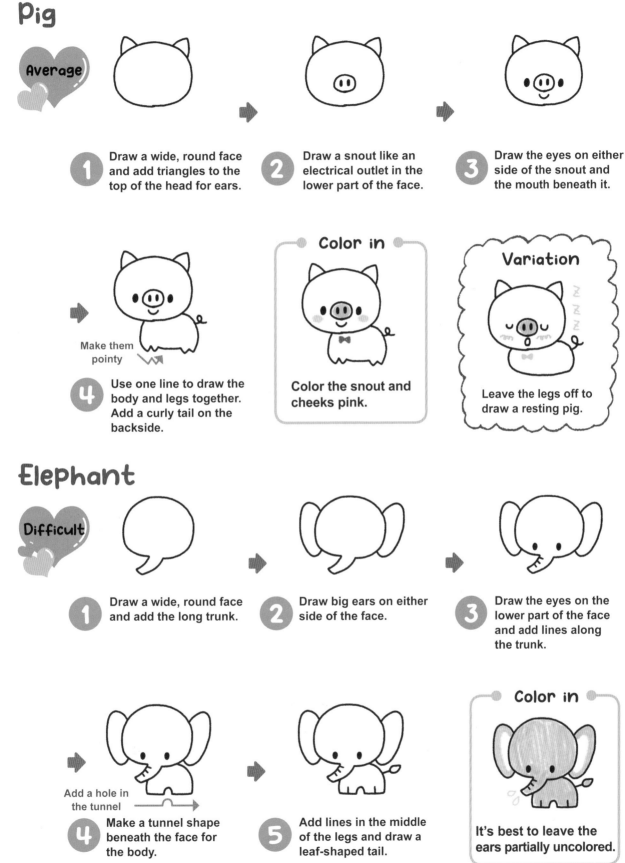

Average

1 Draw a wide, round face and add triangles to the top of the head for ears.

2 Draw a snout like an electrical outlet in the lower part of the face.

3 Draw the eyes on either side of the snout and the mouth beneath it.

Make them pointy

4 Use one line to draw the body and legs together. Add a curly tail on the backside.

Color in
Color the snout and cheeks pink.

Variation
Leave the legs off to draw a resting pig.

Elephant

Difficult

1 Draw a wide, round face and add the long trunk.

2 Draw big ears on either side of the face.

3 Draw the eyes on the lower part of the face and add lines along the trunk.

Add a hole in the tunnel

4 Make a tunnel shape beneath the face for the body.

5 Add lines in the middle of the legs and draw a leaf-shaped tail.

Color in
It's best to leave the ears partially uncolored.

Chick

Easy

1. Draw a shape like a mountain for the head.

2. Join the body to the head.

Make this pointy

3. Draw the eyes and the diamond-shaped beak in the lower half of the face.

4. Add fluffy wings and the legs.

Color in

Color in yellow all over.

Variation

Saying "hello!" from inside the egg. Use zigzags for the broken shell.

Sheep

Easy

Make a rounded square

1. Draw the fleecy bangs and add a rounded square underneath for the face.

2. Draw the eyes, nose and mouth onto the face. Use a line to connect the mouth and nose.

3. Draw coils on either side of the face.

4. Draw fleece all around the face for the body.

5. Draw two sets of legs onto the body and add the springy tail.

Color in

I made the face and legs pink and the horns yellow.

Hamster

Difficult

Join the ears to the face

1 Make a wide, round face and ears using one line. Leave it open at the jawline.

2 Draw the rounded body connected to the face.

3 Draw the eyes, nose and mouth in the lower part of the face. Use a line to join the nose and mouth.

4 Add the feet and hands.

Color in
Use brown to make markings on one ear and on the body.

Variation
You can make it hold a sunflower seed too!

Penguin

Difficult

1 Draw a wide, round face and add a heart-shaped line on the forehead.

2 Draw the eyes and wide beak in the lower part of the face.

3 Draw the urn-shaped body beneath the face.

4 Draw the wings on both sides of the body and the wavy-edged flippers underneath.

Color in
Color the head and wings blue for a realistic look.

Variation
Color the head black and the body gray to create a different species of penguin.

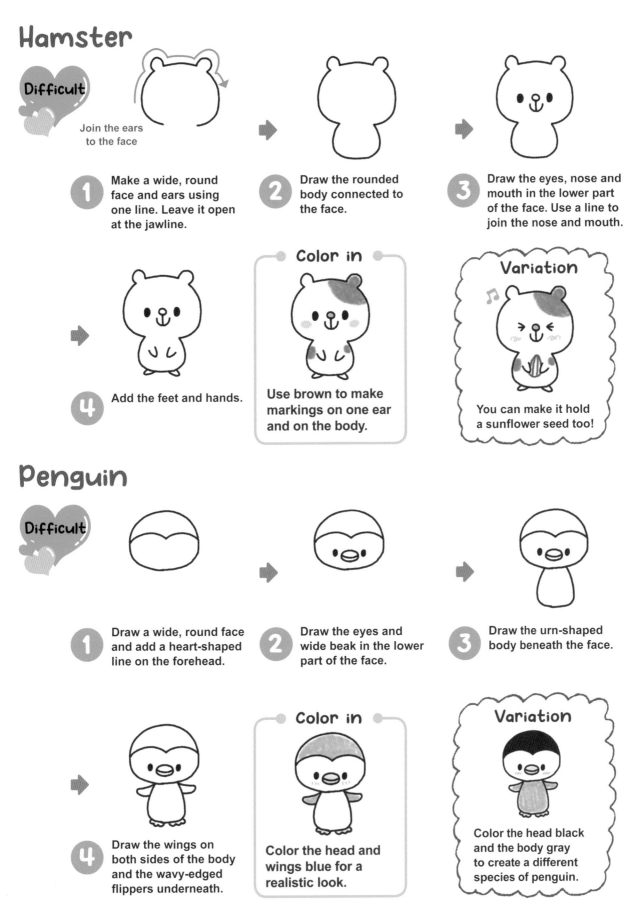

Let's Draw Insects

Now let's turn to bugs and creepy crawlies. They get even cuter once they're captured as Kawaii charmers.

> Some insects fly through the air, some crawl on the ground. Their bodies are all different, and that's what makes them interesting.

Ladybug

Easy

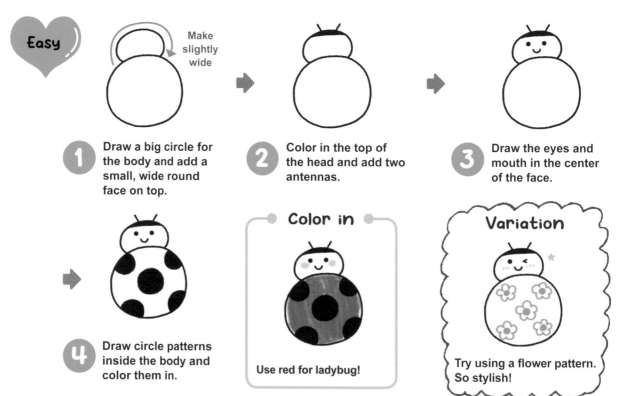

Make slightly wide

1 Draw a big circle for the body and add a small, wide round face on top.

2 Color in the top of the head and add two antennas.

3 Draw the eyes and mouth in the center of the face.

4 Draw circle patterns inside the body and color them in.

Color in

Use red for ladybug!

Variation

Try using a flower pattern. So stylish!

Butterfly

1 Draw a wide, round face and add a long, rounded body beneath it.

2 Draw the eyes and mouth in the lower part of the face and add antennas with round tips on top of the head.

Draw a large curve and a small curve

3 Draw wings on both sides of the body.

4 Add stripes on the lower half of the body and draw three legs on each side.

Variation

Use a heart pattern on the wings to make a butterfly from fairyland!

Bee

1 Draw a wide, round face and add a wide, round body on the right edge.

2 Draw the eyes and mouth in the lower part of the face and add antennas with round tips on top of the head.

Draw a large curve and a small curve

3 Add wings on top of the body.

4 Add stripes to the right half of the body and add lines for the legs and stinger.

Color in

Color the whole bee yellow. Using pale blue for the wings makes them look thin and transparent.

Caterpillar

Easy

1 Draw a wide, round face and add a wide, circle underneath.

2 Add another circle at the lower right.

Make it slightly smaller

3 Add another circle to the lower right edge of the last circle.

4 Draw the eyes and mouth in the lower part of the face and add antennas on top of the head.

Color in
Use yellow and green for a happy, two-tone look!

Variation
I used a bow pattern to create a Kawaii look.

Bagworm

Easy

1 Draw a wide, round face and add the eyes, eyebrows and mouth.

Make the end pointed

2 Draw half of the body, using a scalloped line and tapering a bit toward the bottom.

3 Draw the other half in the same way.

4 Add a line on top of the head and draw leaves over the body.

Color in
Use brown and make scribbly lines to create a dry, rustly effect.

Variation
Coloring only the leaves makes for a stylish effect.

Dragonfly

Average

Draw from the edge of the eyes

1 Draw circles and add circles inside them, coloring them in to create eyes.

2 Draw the face beneath the eyes, making a U shape for the mouth.

3 Draw the long, thin body beneath the head and add stripes in the bottom half.

4 Draw two wings on each side of the body.

Color in
Make the face and body the same color and use pale blue for the wings.

Variation
If you draw spirals inside the eyes, it has the fun effect of making the dragonfly look dizzy.

Snail

Average

1 Draw a spiral.

2 Draw the body next to the spiral.

Make it pointed

3 Draw the eyes and mouth.

4 Add antennas with rounded tips.

Color in
Color only the line of the spiral brown.

Variation
I used a polka dot pattern and added a bow for a dressed-up look.

Let's Draw Sea Creatures

Now it's time to head under the sea for
a class in Kawaii aquatics!

Use blue, light
blue, red and other
colors for the
different creatures.

Fish

Easy

Fish

1 Draw a leaf shape for the body.

2 Add a triangle for the tail.

Add a curved line

3 Draw the eyes and mouth, add a curved line and draw the fin.

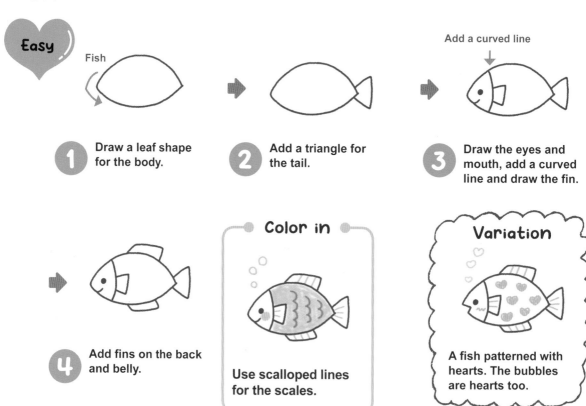

4 Add fins on the back and belly.

Color in

Use scalloped lines for the scales.

Variation

A fish patterned with hearts. The bubbles are hearts too.

Goldfish

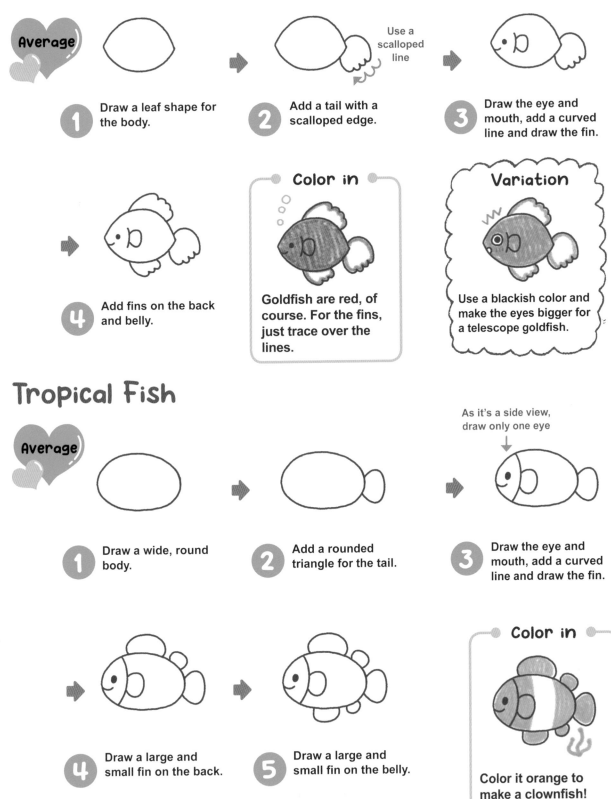

Average

1 Draw a leaf shape for the body.

2 Add a tail with a scalloped edge.

Use a scalloped line

3 Draw the eye and mouth, add a curved line and draw the fin.

4 Add fins on the back and belly.

Color in

Goldfish are red, of course. For the fins, just trace over the lines.

Variation

Use a blackish color and make the eyes bigger for a telescope goldfish.

Tropical Fish

Average

1 Draw a wide, round body.

2 Add a rounded triangle for the tail.

As it's a side view, draw only one eye

3 Draw the eye and mouth, add a curved line and draw the fin.

4 Draw a large and small fin on the back.

5 Draw a large and small fin on the belly.

Color in

Color it orange to make a clownfish!

Shell

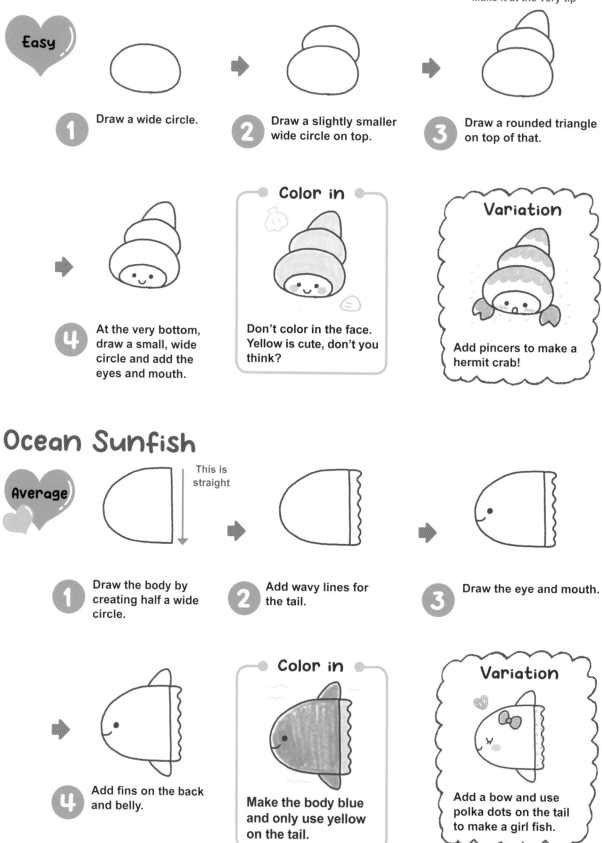

Easy

1. Draw a wide circle.

2. Draw a slightly smaller wide circle on top.

Make it at the very tip

3. Draw a rounded triangle on top of that.

4. At the very bottom, draw a small, wide circle and add the eyes and mouth.

Color in
Don't color in the face. Yellow is cute, don't you think?

Variation
Add pincers to make a hermit crab!

Ocean Sunfish

Average

1. Draw the body by creating half a wide circle.

This is straight

2. Add wavy lines for the tail.

3. Draw the eye and mouth.

4. Add fins on the back and belly.

Color in
Make the body blue and only use yellow on the tail.

Variation
Add a bow and use polka dots on the tail to make a girl fish.

Whale

Average

1. Draw a mountain shape for the back.

   Make it slightly curved

2. Draw a line from the mouth to the tail, leaving it slightly open.

3. Draw the tail on the end.

4. Draw the eye, mouth and fin.

● Color in ●

Leave from below the mouth to the belly uncolored.

Variation

Draw scalloped lines for the water and spray coming out of the back.

Dolphin

Difficult

1. Draw a mountain shape for the back.

   Slightly swell out

2. Draw a line from the mouth to the tail, leaving it slightly open.

3. Add the tail on the end.

4. Add fins on the back and belly.

5. Draw the eye and mouth.

● Color in ●

A fresh pale blue is a good color. Add a beach ball too.

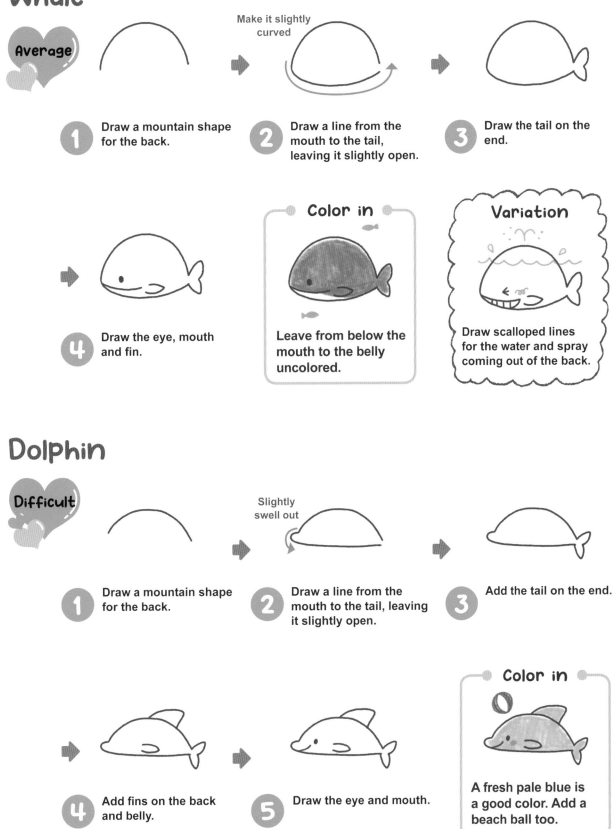

Jellyfish

Easy

It's a slightly squashed circle

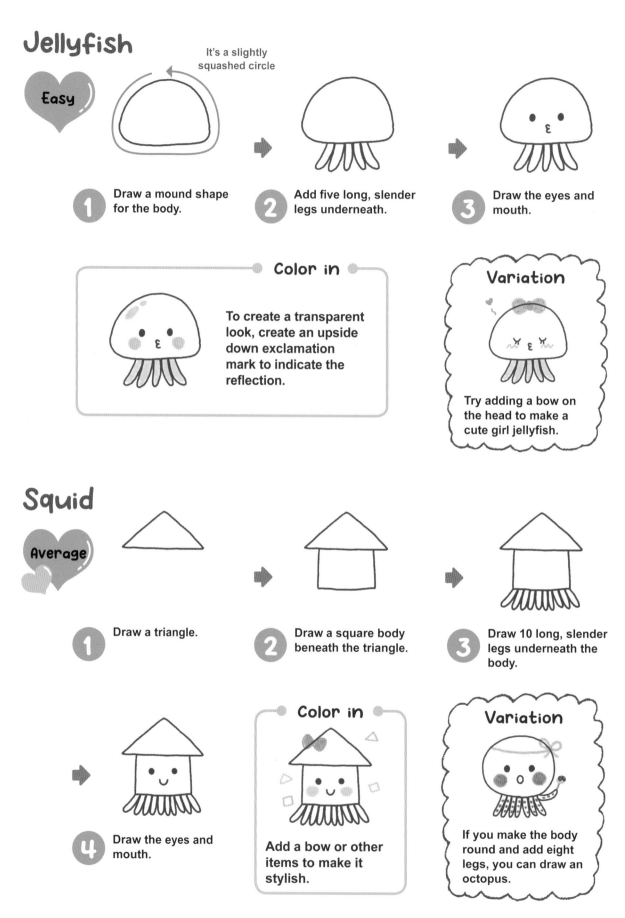

1 Draw a mound shape for the body.

2 Add five long, slender legs underneath.

3 Draw the eyes and mouth.

Color in

To create a transparent look, create an upside down exclamation mark to indicate the reflection.

Variation

Try adding a bow on the head to make a cute girl jellyfish.

Squid

Average

1 Draw a triangle.

2 Draw a square body beneath the triangle.

3 Draw 10 long, slender legs underneath the body.

4 Draw the eyes and mouth.

Color in

Add a bow or other items to make it stylish.

Variation

If you make the body round and add eight legs, you can draw an octopus.

Turtle

Average

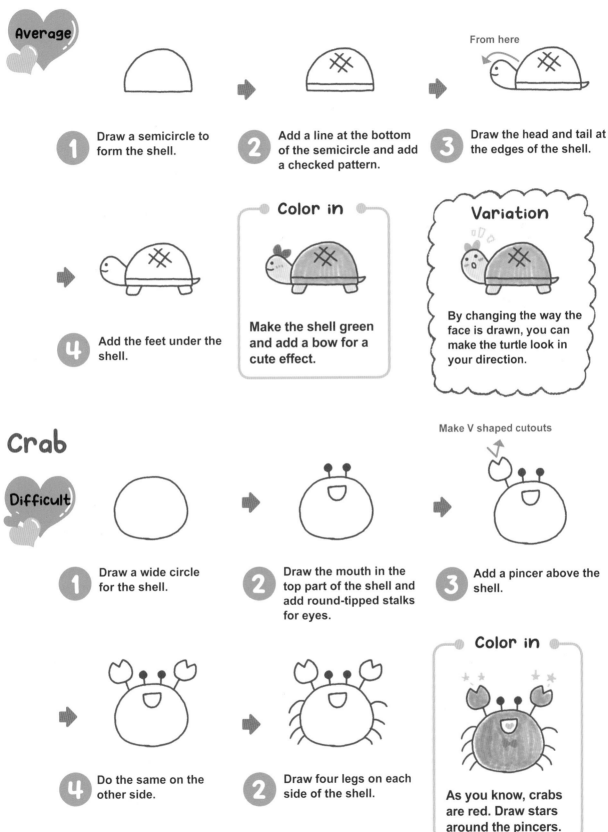

1 Draw a semicircle to form the shell.

2 Add a line at the bottom of the semicircle and add a checked pattern.

3 Draw the head and tail at the edges of the shell.

From here

4 Add the feet under the shell.

Color in

Make the shell green and add a bow for a cute effect.

Variation

By changing the way the face is drawn, you can make the turtle look in your direction.

Crab

Difficult

1 Draw a wide circle for the shell.

2 Draw the mouth in the top part of the shell and add round-tipped stalks for eyes.

3 Add a pincer above the shell.

Make V shaped cutouts

4 Do the same on the other side.

2 Draw four legs on each side of the shell.

Color in

As you know, crabs are red. Draw stars around the pincers.

Let's Draw Kawaii Characters

Have you ever thought of characters that would be fun to have around? Let your imagination loose and create your own original characters!

Try adding faces and limbs to cute motifs like ice cream cones and mushrooms. See? They've become Kawaii characters!

Ice Cream Cone

Average

1 Draw a partially complete wide circle.

2 Join the edges with a scalloped line.

3 Draw the eyes and mouth.

Make it pointy

4 Draw a triangle for the cone underneath the scalloped line.

5 Add matchstick-like arms and legs on either side of the cone.

Color in

Add sprinkles to the head and a grid pattern to the cone.

Mr. Acorn

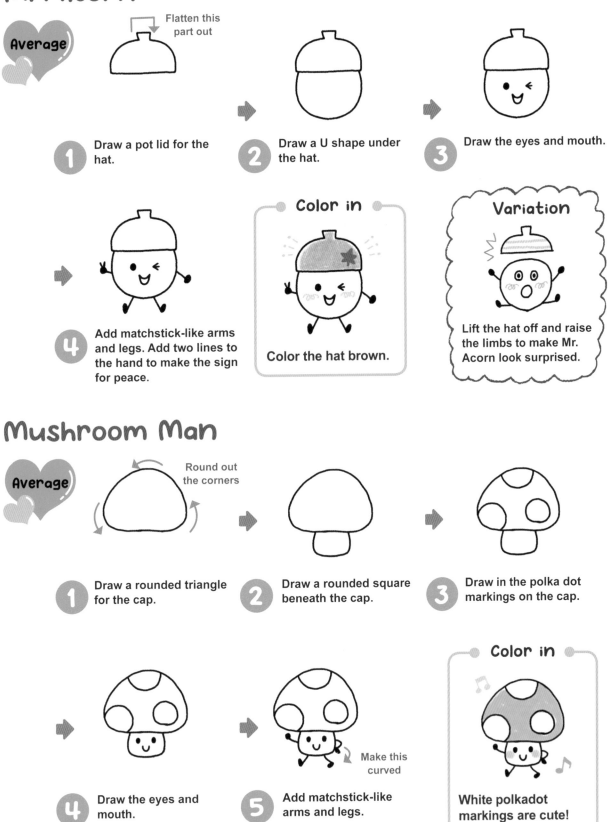

Average

Flatten this part out

1 Draw a pot lid for the hat.

2 Draw a U shape under the hat.

3 Draw the eyes and mouth.

4 Add matchstick-like arms and legs. Add two lines to the hand to make the sign for peace.

● **Color in** ●
Color the hat brown.

Variation
Lift the hat off and raise the limbs to make Mr. Acorn look surprised.

Mushroom Man

Average

Round out the corners

1 Draw a rounded triangle for the cap.

2 Draw a rounded square beneath the cap.

3 Draw in the polka dot markings on the cap.

4 Draw the eyes and mouth.

5 Add matchstick-like arms and legs.

Make this curved

● **Color in** ●
White polkadot markings are cute!

Let's Draw Animal Characters

Here, cute animals are transformed into Kawaii characters. What's your favorite animal? Start with that and go from there!

The faces are animal faces, but the bodies are the same as for humans. Use different tails and ears to create a range of animal friends!

Fluffy Rabbit

Average

1 Draw a wide, round face and add long slender ears on top of the head.

2 Draw a triangle beneath the face for a dress.

3 Draw the eyes, nose and mouth in the lower part of the face.

Make the hands rounded

4 Draw the arms on both sides of the dress and add legs underneath.

Color in
A completely pink rabbit. Isn't she cute?

Variation
Dress the rabbit in pants for a boy. Refer to the bear on page 47.

Cute Kitty

 Average

1 Draw a wide, round face and add triangles to the top of the head for ears.

2 Draw a triangle beneath the face for a dress.

3 Draw the eyes, nose, mouth and whiskers in the lower part of the face.

4 Add arms on both sides of the dress, legs underneath and the tail on the side.

Make it long and thin

Color in

Add brown markings. A red vest suits her too.

Variation

Use tabby markings for a boy.

Cuddle Bear

 Difficult

1 Draw a wide, round face and add round ears on top of the head.

2 Draw the body beneath the face. Make the legs as if joining two squares together.

Draw as if joining two squares

3 Draw the eyes, nose and mouth in the lower part of the face. Make a circle around the nose and mouth.

4 Draw the arms on both sides of the body and add the tail on the side. Make a line across the waist.

Color in

Don't forget to color in the tail!

Variation

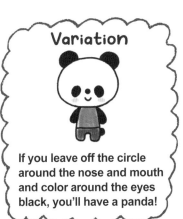

If you leave off the circle around the nose and mouth and color around the eyes black, you'll have a panda!

Dashing Dog

Average

Color in completely

1 Draw a wide, round face and add seed-like shapes for ears on top of the head.

2 Draw a triangle beneath the face to make a dress.

3 Draw the eyes, nose and mouth in the lower part of the face. Draw a circle around the nose and mouth.

4 Draw the arms on both sides of the dress and add legs underneath and a tail on the side.

Color in
Keep it simple and don't use too much color.

Variation
Color brown around one eye. Draw a bone in one paw for a cheeky look.

Plush Pig

Difficult

1 Draw a wide, round face and add triangles for ears.

2 Draw the body beneath the face. Make the legs as if joining two squares together.

3 Draw the eyes, snout and mouth in the lower part of the face.

Make it curly

4 Draw the arms on both sides of the body and add the tail on the side. Make a line across the waist.

Color in
Make the ears and snout the same color.

Variation
For a girl, close the eyes and add a dress.

2

Cute Kawaii Items

Clothes, accessories, cosmetics, interior furnishings. They're all sources of common Kawaii caricatures. Have fun making variations using your own designs and patterns.

Let's Draw Clothes

Have a go at drawing favorite items of clothing, as well as things you wish you could wear. Now don't you feel like a fashion designer?

Add bows and frills to skirts, dresses and T-shirts to make your own designs!

Dress

Easy

1. Draw a long rectangle to make the bodice.

2. Add small squares at each end.

3. Draw the skirt. Make the hem scalloped.

Make it curved for an airy look

4. Draw a bow on the chest and add scalloping above the hem.

Color in

Use pink for the bow and lace to make it cute.

Variation

A musical notes pattern makes for a unique look.

Babydoll Dress

Difficult

Make this square

1. Draw a square with a square section cut out to make the bodice.

2. Draw scalloped lace at the sleeves, a bow on the chest and a line at the waist.

3. Draw the skirt. Make the hem scalloped.

4. Add another layer of scalloping to create two tiers.

Color in

It's fun to use different colors for the bodice and skirt!

Variation

Make the sleeves rounded for puff sleeves. Add big bows to the skirt.

Princess Dress

Difficult

Make this rounded

1. Draw a square with a round section cut out to make the bodice.

2. Draw the rounded sleeves and scalloping over the chest and draw a line across the waist.

3. Draw the skirt. Create large scalloping along the hem.

4. Add fine scalloping below the hem to create two tiers.

Color in

Use a different color for the waist and ribbons for a gorgeous effect.

Variation

I added a scoop and decorated it with a rose.

Flared Skirt

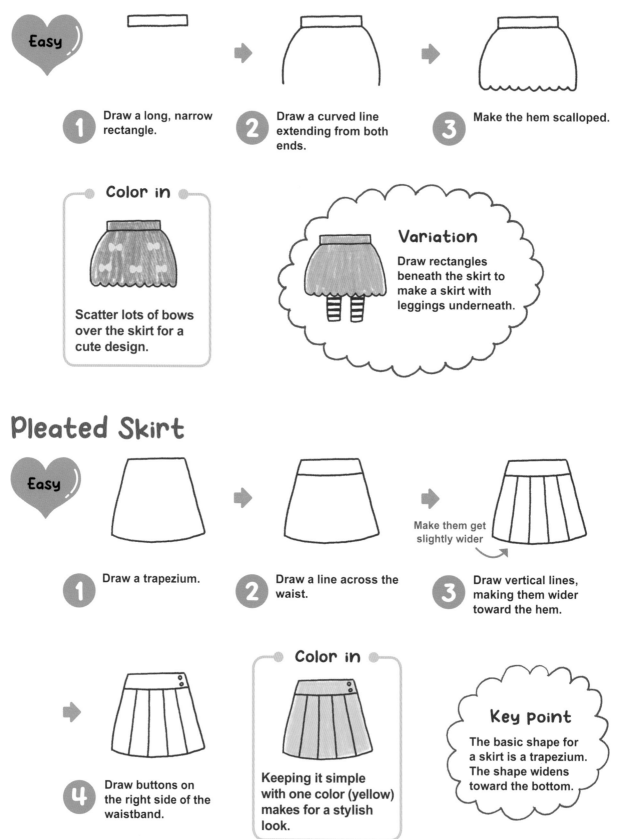

Easy

1. Draw a long, narrow rectangle.

2. Draw a curved line extending from both ends.

3. Make the hem scalloped.

Color in

Scatter lots of bows over the skirt for a cute design.

Variation

Draw rectangles beneath the skirt to make a skirt with leggings underneath.

Pleated Skirt

Easy

1. Draw a trapezium.

2. Draw a line across the waist.

3. Draw vertical lines, making them wider toward the hem.

Make them get slightly wider

4. Draw buttons on the right side of the waistband.

Color in

Keeping it simple with one color (yellow) makes for a stylish look.

Key point

The basic shape for a skirt is a trapezium. The shape widens toward the bottom.

Shorts

Average

1 Draw a bow.

2 Draw lines from both sides of the bow to make the waist.

3 From the waist, draw two squares connecting.

Make a small cutout

4 Draw a horizontal line across the waist.

Color in

I drew pockets and added lace at the hems.

Variation

Remove the center bow and add bows on both sides to make things simpler.

Jeans

Difficult

1 Draw a horizontal line for the waist.

2 From the waist, draw a narrow rectangle.

Up to here

3 Do the same on the other side and join them.

4 Draw lines across the waist and hems and add a round button.

5 Draw a narrow rectangle beneath the button and add pockets on both sides.

Color in

Color them blue to make them look like real denim.

T-Shirt

Easy

1 Make a semicircle for the collar.

2 Draw square sleeves from both ends of the collar.

3 Draw a square to connect the underarms.

4 Decorate with bows.

Color in
Leave the T-shirt white, and make the bows colorful.

Variation
Use stars for the pattern and add frilly lace around the hem!

Sweater

Average

1 Draw the collar.

Create a curve

2 Draw the long sleeves connected to the collar.

3 Draw a square to connect the underarms.

4 Add vertical lines in the collar, hem and sleeves.

Color in
This cute heart pattern will beat the winter cold!

Key point
For soft clothing like sweaters, make the corners rounded rather than sharp. This will make for a soft, plush look.

Coat

Average

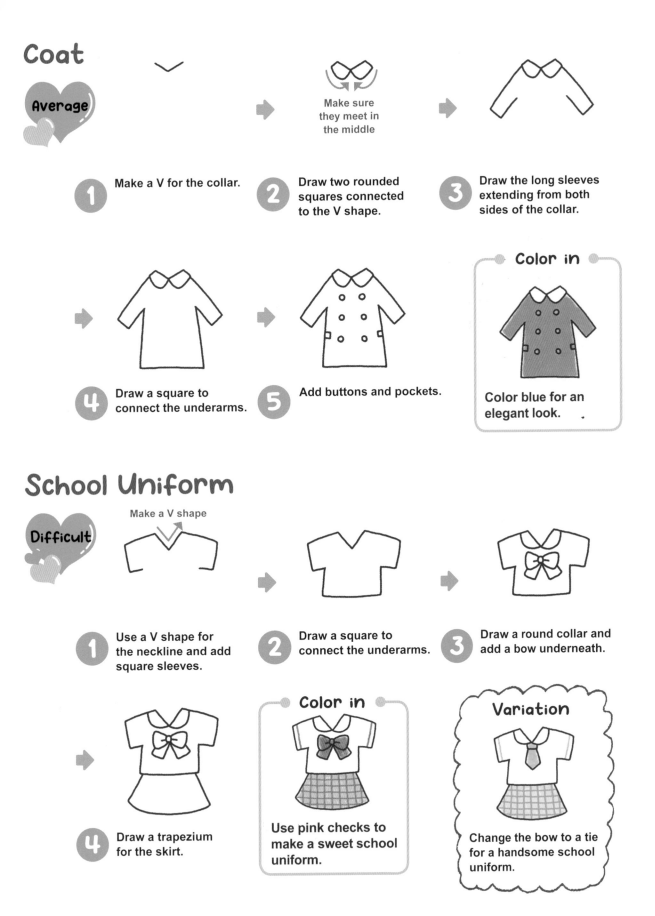

1. Make a V for the collar.

Make sure they meet in the middle

2. Draw two rounded squares connected to the V shape.

3. Draw the long sleeves extending from both sides of the collar.

4. Draw a square to connect the underarms.

5. Add buttons and pockets.

Color in

Color blue for an elegant look.

School Uniform

Difficult

Make a V shape

1. Use a V shape for the neckline and add square sleeves.

2. Draw a square to connect the underarms.

3. Draw a round collar and add a bow underneath.

4. Draw a trapezium for the skirt.

Color in

Use pink checks to make a sweet school uniform.

Variation

Change the bow to a tie for a handsome school uniform.

Let's Draw Stylish Items

Hats, accessories, cosmetics … these fashionable items are perfect for a Kawaii makeover.

Use whatever pattern you like to make variations. Play around with different designs.

Headband

Easy

1 Draw a bow.

2 Add frilly lace on each edge of the bow.

Color it in to make it thicker

3 Draw a curve from the side of the bow.

4 Do the same on the other side.

Color in

Color in pink and add blue polka dots.

Variation

Layer a small and big heart on as decorations.

Beret

Easy

1 Draw a wide, round shape without joining the ends.

2 Draw a horizontal line to connect the ends.

3 Draw the flower decoration and a narrow oval on the top of the hat.

Color in

The purple color is so grown up! It works well with the yellow flower.

Variation

Try putting a fluffy ball on top of the hat. It's just right for winter fashions!

Hat

Average

1 Draw a bow.

2 Draw a mountain shape extending from the bow.

Make this longer

3 Draw a narrow brim.

4 Add a narrow band.

Color in

Color the bow a bright red to catch the eye.

Variation

Horizontal stripes make for a stylish look.

Purse

Easy

1 Draw a square with rounded corners.

Make it big

2 Draw two curved lines from either side of the square to form the shoulder strap.

3 Draw a large heart with a bow in the middle.

Color in

Pink and green are a perfect Kawaii color combination!

Variation

Add a semicircle to make a purse with a flap.

Bag

Average

1 Draw a semicircle.

Draw so the thickness doesn't change

2 Draw two curved lines on top of the semicircle for the handles.

3 Draw a scalloped line at the bottom of the bag.

4 Add two bows beneath the handles.

Color in

I used a polka dot pattern on the lower portion.

Variation

Hang a heart-shaped tag from the handle. Don't forget the cord!

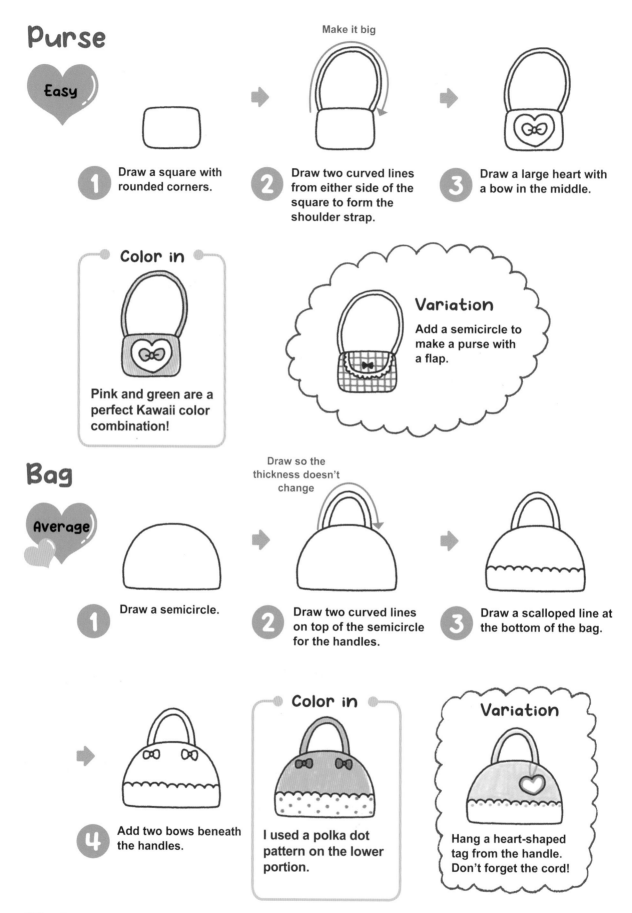

Shoes

Easy

Make the line slightly diagonal

1 Draw a curved line.

2 Draw a vertical line at the end of the curved line.

3 Draw a curved line from the other end and connect it to the vertical line.

4 Draw another shoe in the same way.

○ **Color in** ○

Add lace for a subtle, refined look.

Variation

For sneakers, add lines at the toes and heel, and for pumps, add a heel.

Socks

Easy

Make this long

1 Draw a frilly line.

2 Draw vertical lines coming down from the frilly line.

3 Draw a curve to connect the vertical lines.

4 Add a line in the heel and draw the other sock in the same way.

○ **Color in** ○

Add lots of small hearts.

Variation

It's easy to draw the top of the sock folded over.

Long Boots

Easy

1 Draw a horizontal line.

2 Draw vertical lines from both sides of the horizontal line.

Make this part longer

3 Draw a curve to connect the vertical lines.

4 Draw a horizontal line on the bottom of the boot. Draw the other boot in the same way.

Color in
Draw a polka dot pattern for a cute look.

Variation
Try adding a fleecy trim to create sheepskin boots.

Umbrella

Average

1 Draw a mountain-like shape.

2 Join the edges with a scalloped line. Add a dot on the pointed sections.

3 Draw a small circle on the top and a thick line underneath to make the stem.

Color in to thicken

4 Add a J shape for the handle.

Color in
A musical note pattern makes rainy days fun.

Variation
For a closed umbrella, make a long narrow triangle.

Scarf

Easy

1 Draw a long rectangle with rounded corners.

2 Draw a square at the lower right.

3 Draw a heart.

4 Draw vertical lines at the end.

Color in

Use a color close to that of the scarf itself to draw the stitches for a realistic look. Use scribbly lines to color the heart and create the look of a fabric patch.

Mittens

Easy

1 Draw a horizontal line.

Large curve and small curve

2 Draw a heart shape to join both sides of the horizontal line.

3 Draw the other mitten in the same way.

4 Draw a line with a curl in the middle to join the two mittens together.

Color in

Color in, leaving the scalloped section in the middle plain.

Key point

When drawing the heart shape in step **2**, make the thumb section small and the section for the remaining four fingers large.

Glasses

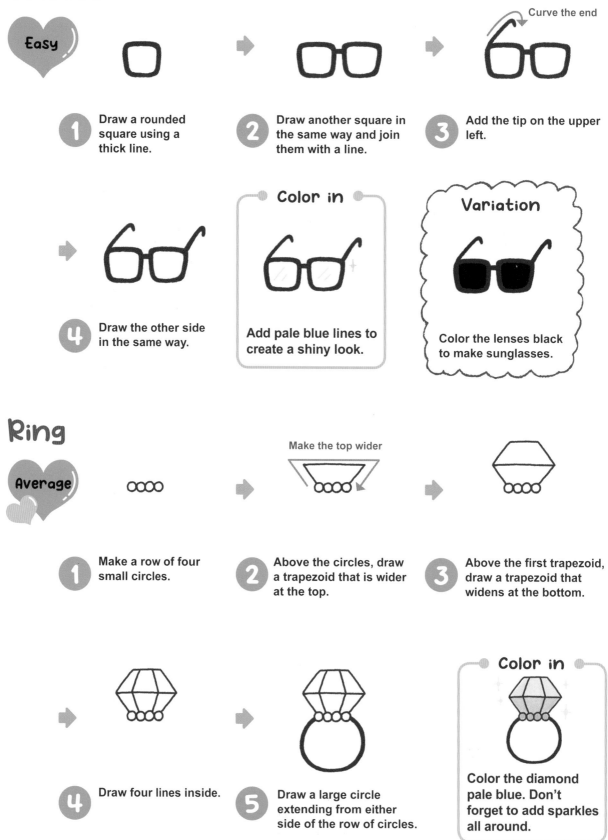

Easy

1. Draw a rounded square using a thick line.

2. Draw another square in the same way and join them with a line.

3. Add the tip on the upper left.

Curve the end

4. Draw the other side in the same way.

Color in

Add pale blue lines to create a shiny look.

Variation

Color the lenses black to make sunglasses.

Ring

Average

1. Make a row of four small circles.

2. Above the circles, draw a trapezoid that is wider at the top.

Make the top wider

3. Above the first trapezoid, draw a trapezoid that widens at the bottom.

4. Draw four lines inside.

5. Draw a large circle extending from either side of the row of circles.

Color in

Color the diamond pale blue. Don't forget to add sparkles all around.

Necklace

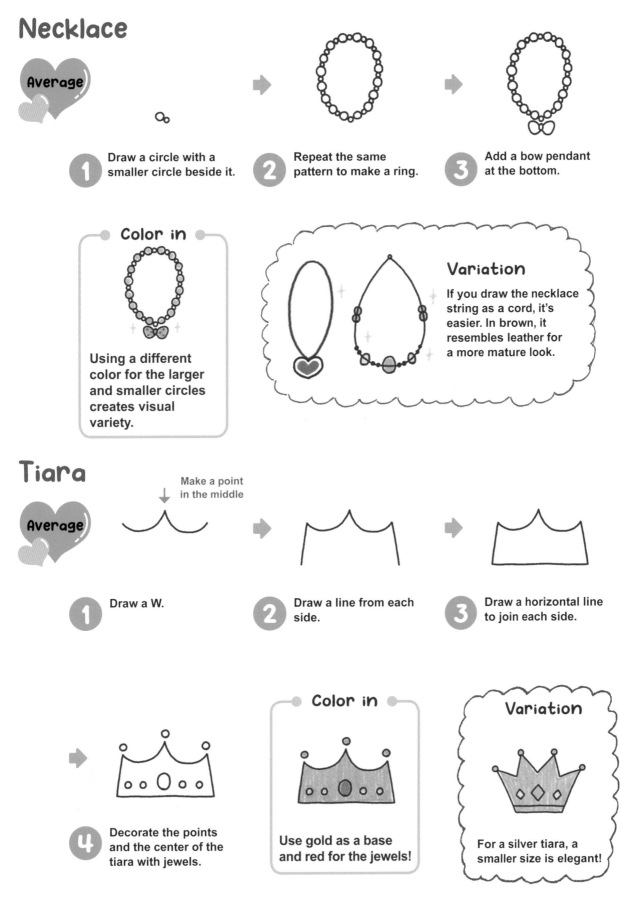

Average

1 Draw a circle with a smaller circle beside it.

2 Repeat the same pattern to make a ring.

3 Add a bow pendant at the bottom.

Color in

Using a different color for the larger and smaller circles creates visual variety.

Variation

If you draw the necklace string as a cord, it's easier. In brown, it resembles leather for a more mature look.

Tiara

Average

Make a point in the middle

1 Draw a W.

2 Draw a line from each side.

3 Draw a horizontal line to join each side.

4 Decorate the points and the center of the tiara with jewels.

Color in

Use gold as a base and red for the jewels!

Variation

For a silver tiara, a smaller size is elegant!

Nail Polish

Easy

1 Draw a rectangle.

2 Draw an urn shape under the rectangle.

Make this straight →

3 Draw a heart with an upside-down exclamation mark to the left above it.

Color in

Color in the liquid inside, leaving a bit uncolored around the edge.

Variation

Make the bottle square and fill in with lots of different colors. Drawing the bottle with the cap off creates a unique look.

Perfume

Average

1 Draw a row of small circles.

2 Draw a heart above the circles.

3 Draw an urn shape underneath.

Draw a curve that tapers in at the bottom.

4 Draw an upside-down exclamation mark to the upper left.

Color in

Color the perfume in the bottle yellow, leaving a little uncolored on the inside edge for a realistic effect.

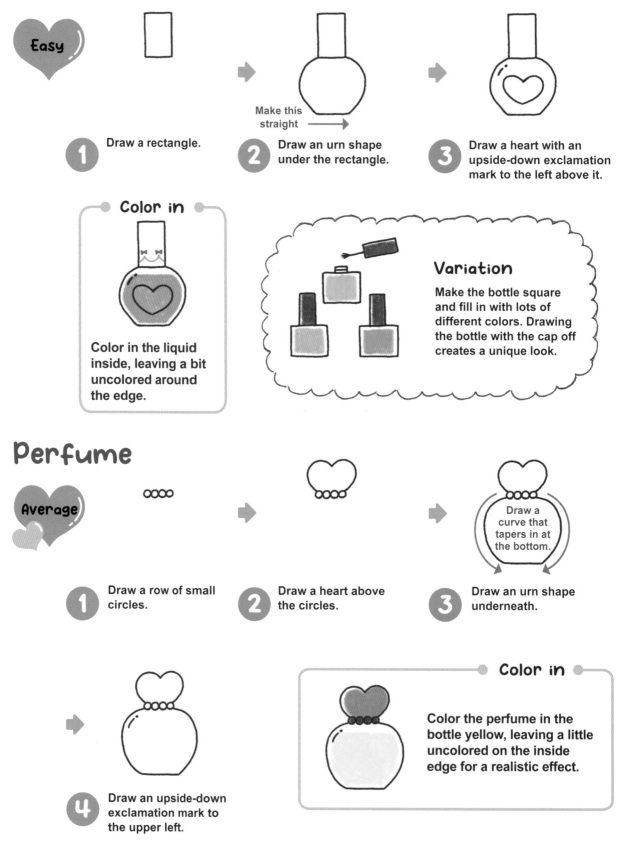

Lip Balm

Difficult

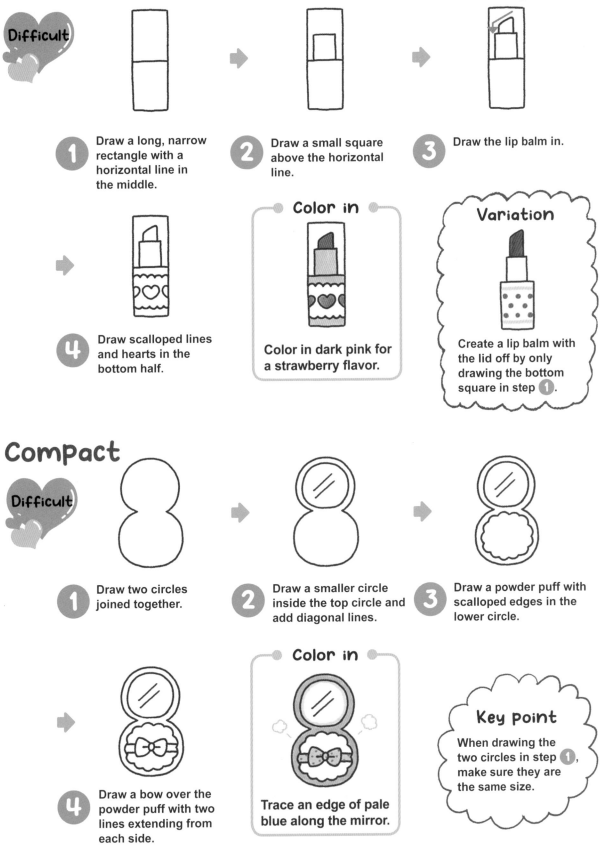

Draw a diagonal line

1 Draw a long, narrow rectangle with a horizontal line in the middle.

2 Draw a small square above the horizontal line.

3 Draw the lip balm in.

4 Draw scalloped lines and hearts in the bottom half.

Color in

Color in dark pink for a strawberry flavor.

Variation

Create a lip balm with the lid off by only drawing the bottom square in step **1**.

Compact

Difficult

1 Draw two circles joined together.

2 Draw a smaller circle inside the top circle and add diagonal lines.

3 Draw a powder puff with scalloped edges in the lower circle.

4 Draw a bow over the powder puff with two lines extending from each side.

Color in

Trace an edge of pale blue along the mirror.

Key point

When drawing the two circles in step **1**, make sure they are the same size.

Let's Draw Favorite Furnishings

It's time to upgrade your Kawaii style, with these oh-so-cute versions of things you'd find in and around your home.

Even large items such as desks and sofas are easy to draw if you take a good look at the examples.

Garden Tree

Easy

1 Draw a circular shape that's not perfectly round.

Draw a zigzag

2 Draw the trunk beneath the circle shape. Make the bottom a zigzag line.

3 Draw vertical lines inside the trunk and add a little branch on the side.

4 Draw the leaves.

Color in
Use light and dark green to color the leaves.

Variation
Make the outline scalloped and add apples if you like.

House

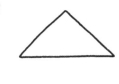

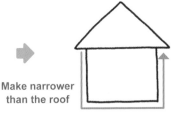

1 Draw a triangle for the roof.

Make narrower than the roof

2 Draw a square beneath the triangle.

3 On the bottom right of the square, draw a rectangle for a door and add a doorknob.

4 In the upper left, draw a square with a cross in it for a wooden window frame. Make only the bottom line thick.

Color in

The red roof looks like something from a fairy tale, doesn't it?

Variation

Use a trapezium for the roof to add variety to the basic shape.

Planter Box

1 Draw a square for the planter box. Add a scalloped line at the top.

2 Above the box, draw a flower using a circle with a scalloped line around it.

3 Connect the flower and the box with a vertical line for the stem.

4 Draw leaves on both sides of the stem.

Color in

Color in the petals.

Variation

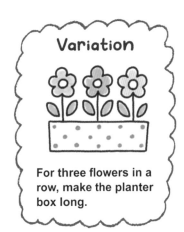

For three flowers in a row, make the planter box long.

Lamp

Average

1. Draw a mesa-shaped mound.

2. Use a scalloped line to connect the bottom and create the lampshade.

3. Draw a stand with a triangular shape at the base.

Create a slight curve

4. Draw a line of dots and a bow under the shade.

Color in

Use bows and dots to decorate the lampshade for a romantic effect. Drawing yellow lines under the shade makes it look like the light is on.

Desk

Average

1. Draw a long, thin rectangle.

2. Beneath one end, draw a leg with a circle at the bottom.

3. Draw the other leg in the same way.

4. Add decoration by drawing a scalloped line between the two legs.

5. Add a flower-shaped handle above the scalloping.

Color in

It looks best if the flower-shaped handle is a different color from the rest of the desk.

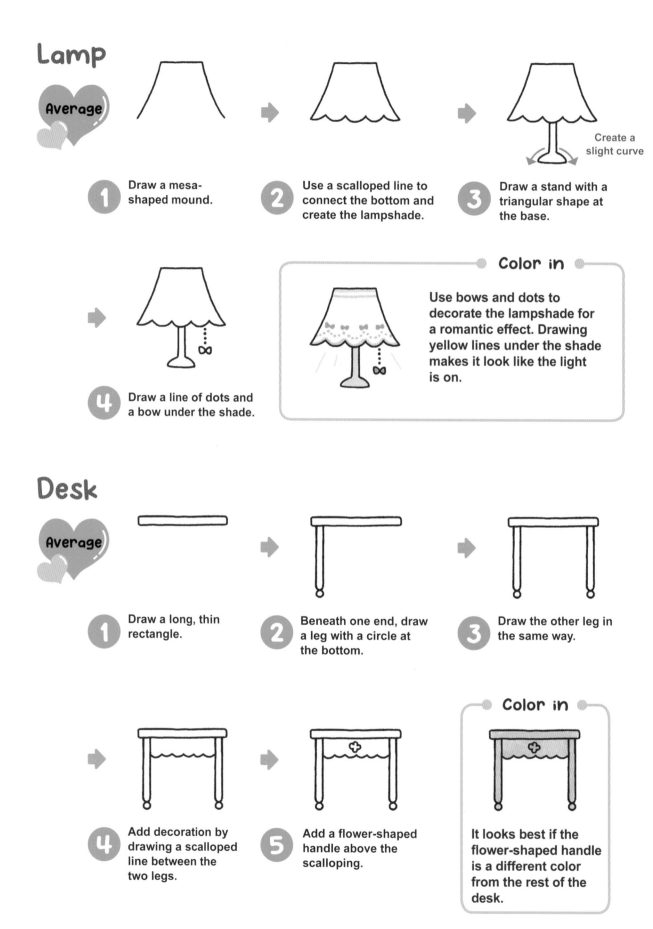

Chair

Average

Make the ends rounded

1 Draw a long, thin rectangle.

2 Draw the legs at each end of the rectangle.

3 Add the seat back at the end of the rectangle and add a circle at the top.

4 Add a scalloped line for decoration to join the legs.

Color in
Color in a light brown to suggest the tone of wood.

Variation
Add a cushion and hang a bag over the back.

Sofa

Difficult

1 Partially draw a rounded square.

Make this part rounded

2 Draw narrow rectangles on each side.

3 Draw a horizontal line at the bottom and add square feet.

4 Add a slightly curved line for the seat.

Color in
Fill in the whole sofa in whatever color you like.

Variation
Make it longer for a three-seater sofa.

Notebook

Easy

1 Draw a rectangle.

2 Draw a vertical line on one side.

3 Draw a rectangle above the center.

4 Draw scalloped lines for decoration at the top and bottom.

Color in

A vertical stripe pattern works well.

Variation

Draw lots of short lines on the edge to make a spiral-bound notebook!

Pen

Average

1 Draw a long, narrow angled rectangle.

2 Draw a triangle at the end and add a dot for the pointed tip.

3 Add a heart to the end.

Add lines here

4 Add in scalloped lines and the clip.

Color in

Try drawing a curly line from the tip of the pen!

Variation

You can use the same shape to draw a pencil.

Cup

 Easy

1 Draw a bowl shape.

2 On the side of the bowl, add a handle.

3 Draw a narrow rounded shape under the bowl to create a little saucer.

4 Add a bow decoration.

Color in

A cute design makes for a lovely tea time.

Variation

Add handles to both sides to make a soup mug.

Fork & Spoon

Average

1 Draw the spoon by making a circle for the head and extending the handle down from it.

Make rounded

2 Add a long rectangle underneath with the end rounded.

3 Draw the fork. Draw zigzags for the head and extend the handle down from there.

4 Add a long rounded rectangle as before. Add scalloped lines around the handles.

Color in

Cheerful colors like orange and green are eye-catching.

Key point

The fork shape is based on the spoon, just use a zigzag line for the edge.

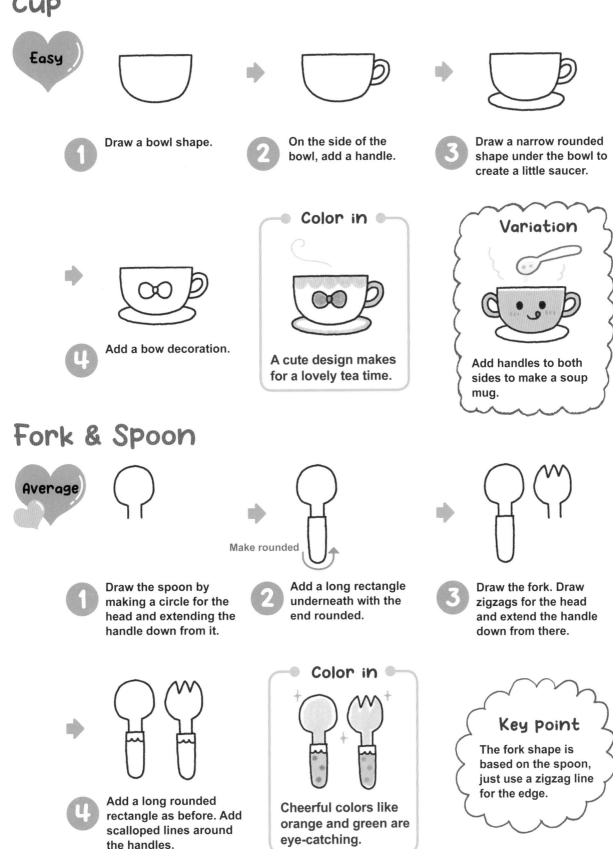

Clock

Easy

1. Draw a circle with another circle inside.

2. Draw a small circle at the center.

3. Draw a vertical line above the small circle.

4. In the same way, draw a short, thick horizontal line from the small circle.

Color in
It's good to add symbols where the numbers are.

Variation
Add small semicircles on top to make an alarm clock!

Teddy Bear

Average

1. Using the bear on page 30 as a reference, draw the face.

2. Draw the arms beneath the face.

Make the ends rounded

3. Draw the legs, extending the line from the underarms.

4. Draw a bow on the chest.

Color in
Make a V-shaped line of dots from the forehead to the nose.

Variation
Use scribbly lines to add color and create a fleecy look.

3 Favorite Kawaii Foods

The Kawaii kitchen is open! Not just sweets and desserts are being given the Kawaii treatment here, but all your favorite foods!

Let's Draw Bread

An entire bakery comes alive with Kawaii kookiness. Everyday favorite foods make perfect subjects.

You can change the fillings for sandwiches to whatever you like. Have fun making a variety!

Baguette

Easy

1 Draw a long, narrow oval.

2 Add a diagonal slash.

3 Add in a line of slashes in the same way.

Color in

Color the bread in dark brown and the slashes in light brown.

Variation

Draw the bread in a paper bag for a stylish look. You could add lettuce and tomato inside to make a sandwich.

Slice of Bread

Easy

1. Draw part of a long oval, leaving it open.

2. Use a square to connect the ends of the oval.

3. **Start from here** — On the right, trace the shape to create the crust.

Color in

Color the outside in dark brown and draw a face.

Variation

You can make all sorts of variations such as spreading strawberry jelly on the bread or creating a wide crust and bagging it.

Sandwich

Average

1. Draw a triangle.

2. Draw a rectangle beneath the triangle. *Make the same width as the triangle*

3. Make two horizontal lines in the middle.

4. Draw a scalloped line under the two lines.

Color in

Color the ham pink and the lettuce green.

Variation

Make a scalloped line in the top as if someone has taken a bite.

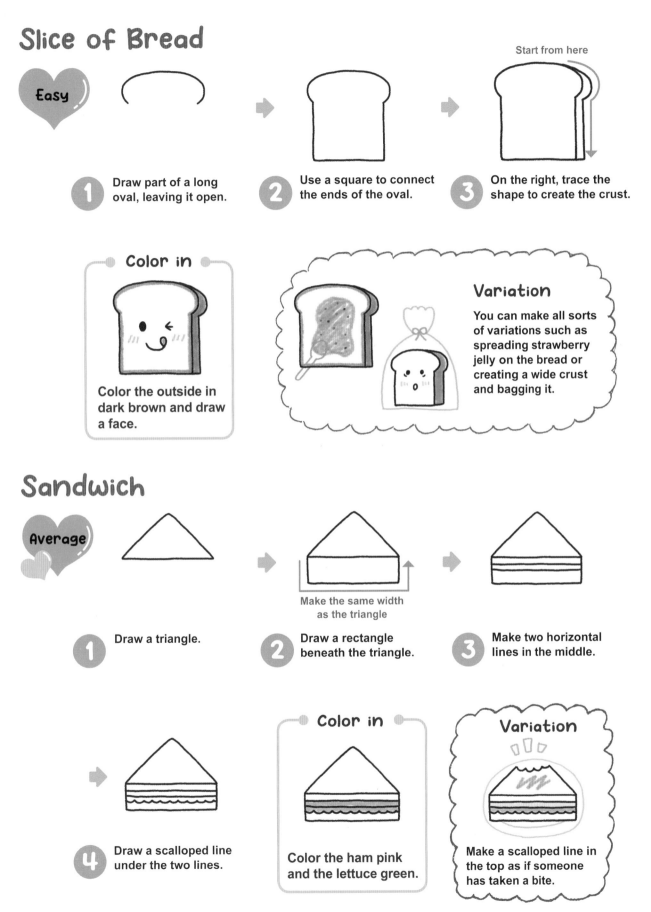

Croissant

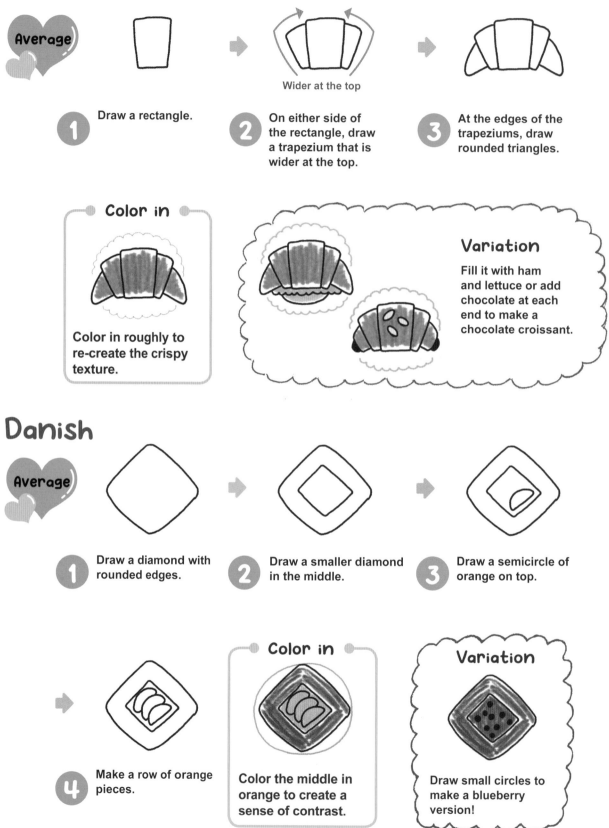

Average

1 Draw a rectangle.

2 On either side of the rectangle, draw a trapezium that is wider at the top.

Wider at the top

3 At the edges of the trapeziums, draw rounded triangles.

Color in

Color in roughly to re-create the crispy texture.

Variation

Fill it with ham and lettuce or add chocolate at each end to make a chocolate croissant.

Danish

Average

1 Draw a diamond with rounded edges.

2 Draw a smaller diamond in the middle.

3 Draw a semicircle of orange on top.

4 Make a row of orange pieces.

Color in

Color the middle in orange to create a sense of contrast.

Variation

Draw small circles to make a blueberry version!

Pizza

Average

1 Draw a circle.

2 On top of the circle, use a wavy line to create cheese.

3 Make flower-like shapes for the pepper.

4 Use little circles to make the pepperoni.

Color in
Color the pepper in green and the pepperoni in red.

Variation
Make a V-shape to show a slice has been cut out.

Hamburger

Difficult

Make curved

1 Draw a semicircle shape for the bread and add sesame seeds.

2 Draw a rounded rectangle underneath to make the patty.

3 Draw a scalloped line beneath the patty to make the lettuce.

4 Draw a rounded rectangle beneath the lettuce.

Color in
Use a different method of filling in color for the bread and the patty.

Variation
Add a rectangle for the tomato and a triangle for the cheese to create a bigger burger!

Let's Draw Desserts

These are Kawaii classics: sweet treats and cute smiling desserts in four easy steps!

Adding color instantly makes things look tasty. Color in only specific parts such as the strawberries or topping for a good result.

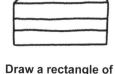

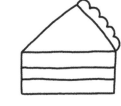

Slice of Cake

 Average

1 Draw a slightly uneven triangle.

2 Draw a rectangle of sponge beneath the triangle and add in two horizontal lines.

3 Draw a trapezium for the cup beneath the scalloping.

4 Draw a strawberry. Add scalloping underneath it,

Color in

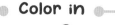

Show slivers of red for the strawberries in between the sponge layers.

Variation

Color dark brown to make a chocolate cake!

Cupcake

Average

1 Draw a circle for the chestnut.

Make a large curve

2 Draw big scalloping from both sides of the chestnut.

3 Draw a trapezium for the cup beneath the scalloping.

4 Add slightly curved lines.

Color in
Use a yellow for the buttercream frosting.

Variation
Use purple icing and a cute decoration on top for a festive touch.

Decorated Cake

Difficult

1 Draw a square with rounded corners, leaving the bottom open.

2 Join the ends with a scalloped line.

3 Draw the square sponge underneath.

Slightly rounded on top

4 Draw three strawberries on top.

Color in
Use white for the cream and yellow for the sponge.

Variation
Add a line of candles to make a birthday cake.

Soda

Easy

1 Draw a trapezium that's wider at the top and add a horizontal line across it.

2 Add a line with a bend in it for the straw.

3 Draw the inner edge of the straw and close off the shape.

Make the same width →

4 Add small circles for the bubbles.

Color in

Color it in green, leaving the bubbles plain.

Variation

Add ice cream and a cherry on top for an ice cream soda.

Pudding

Average

1 Draw a boat-shaped bowl.

Relaxed curve

2 Beneath the bowl, draw a stem with a triangle base.

3 Above the bowl, draw a trapezium.

4 Add a scalloped line at the top of the trapezium.

Color in

Color in yellow, using dark brown above the scalloped line.

Variation

Make the top of the trapezium scalloped to create jello.

Soft Serve Ice Cream

Average

Make a pointed top

1. Draw a scalloped line for one side of the soft serve.

2. Make the top pointy and draw the other side.

3. Draw a trapezium underneath for the cone.

4. Add a hash pattern on the cone.

Color in

I added pink scalloped lines.

Key point

When drawing the scalloping in step 2, start from the pointed tip. Make sure the shape is the same as the other side.

Sundae

Difficult

Make triangular

1. Draw a triangle for the glass. Make a small triangle at the base.

2. Draw a scalloped line for the whipped cream.

3. Add two round scoops of ice cream.

4. Add dots and scalloped lines on top of the ice cream for the toppings.

Color in

Add color inside the glass to show the different layers and add a rectangle with a hash pattern for the wafer!

Donut

Easy

1 Draw a circle.

2 Draw a small circle inside it.

Don't draw inside the small circle

3 Make a scalloped line across the middle.

4 Add tiny circles in the top part.

Color in

Color above the scalloped line in dark brown to make chocolate.

Variation

Play around with various colors and decorations above the scalloping.

Macaron

Easy

1 Draw a mountain-like shape.

2 Connect the ends by creating a swollen rounded shape.

Swell out in a rounded shape

3 Leave some space below the shape and draw the same shape upside down underneath.

4 Draw cream in between the shapes using diagonal lines.

Color in

Cute pink is the perfect color!

Variation

Use all different colors and put them in a bag.

Muffin

Average

1 Draw a scalloped line.

2 Draw a trapezium underneath for the wrapper.

3 Draw a round oval above the scalloping.

4 Add a bow and scalloping inside the oval.

Color in

Make the muffin brown and the icing white. Add colorful dots for cute decoration.

Pancakes

Average

1 Draw a circle.

2 Draw a curve in line with the lower edge.

3 Draw half an oval underneath to create a layer and add the curved line.

Draw half the oval

4 Draw a square of butter on top surrounded with a wavy line.

Color in

Use yellow for the edges for a realistic look! Add scalloped lines for steam.

Let's Draw Fruit and Vegetables

It's time for a healthy snack, Kawaii-style! So many colors to use and choose from!

You can draw them peeled or cut into sections, so there's a lot of options.

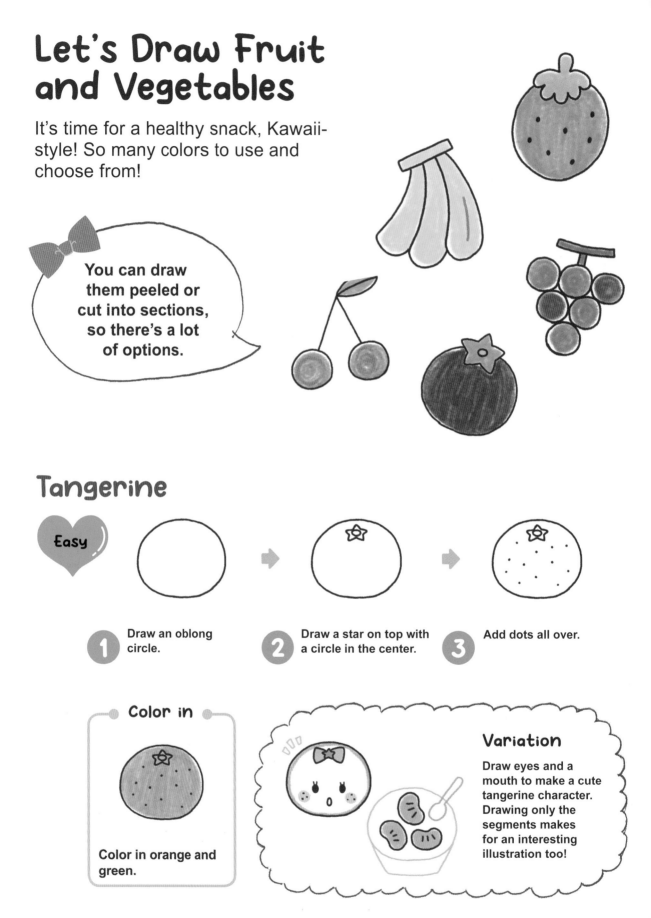

Tangerine

Easy

1 Draw an oblong circle.

2 Draw a star on top with a circle in the center.

3 Add dots all over.

Color in

Color in orange and green.

Variation

Draw eyes and a mouth to make a cute tangerine character. Drawing only the segments makes for an interesting illustration too!

Watermelon

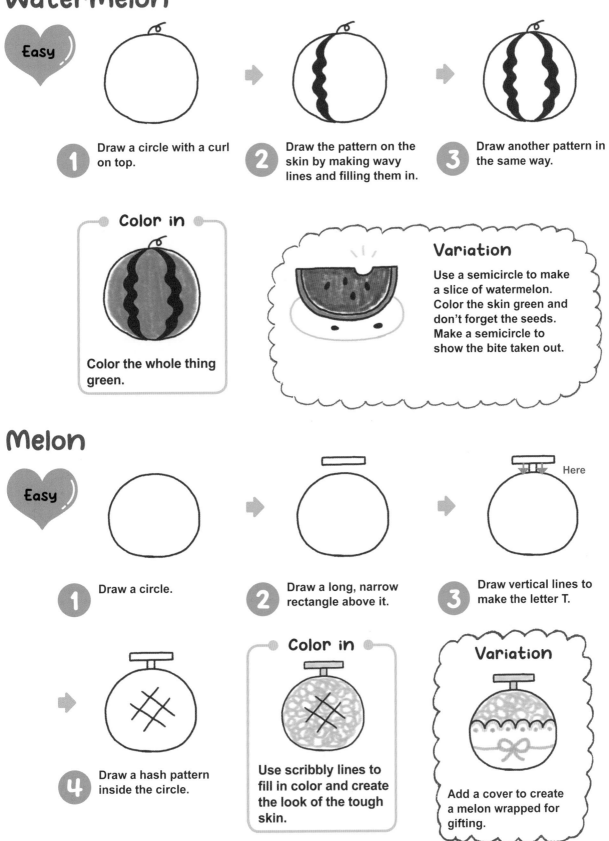

Easy

1 Draw a circle with a curl on top.

2 Draw the pattern on the skin by making wavy lines and filling them in.

3 Draw another pattern in the same way.

Color in

Color the whole thing green.

Variation

Use a semicircle to make a slice of watermelon. Color the skin green and don't forget the seeds. Make a semicircle to show the bite taken out.

Melon

Easy

1 Draw a circle.

2 Draw a long, narrow rectangle above it.

3 Draw vertical lines to make the letter T.

Here

4 Draw a hash pattern inside the circle.

Color in

Use scribbly lines to fill in color and create the look of the tough skin.

Variation

Add a cover to create a melon wrapped for gifting.

Peach

Easy

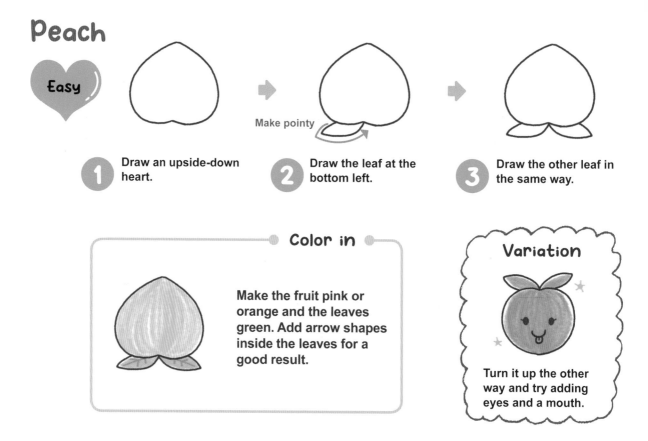

1 Draw an upside-down heart.

Make pointy

2 Draw the leaf at the bottom left.

3 Draw the other leaf in the same way.

Color in

Make the fruit pink or orange and the leaves green. Add arrow shapes inside the leaves for a good result.

Variation

Turn it up the other way and try adding eyes and a mouth.

Apple

Easy

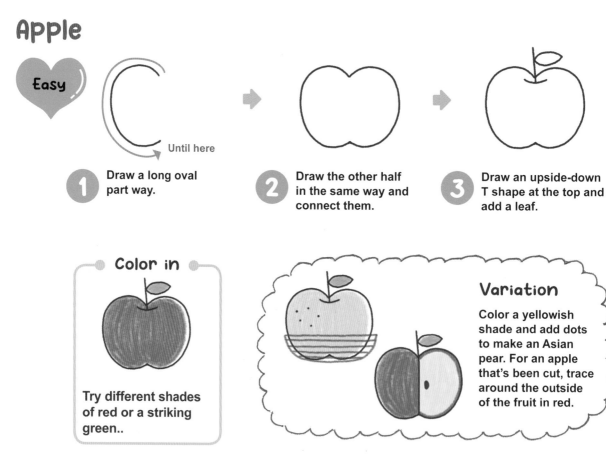

1 Draw a long oval part way.

Until here

2 Draw the other half in the same way and connect them.

3 Draw an upside-down T shape at the top and add a leaf.

Color in

Try different shades of red or a striking green..

Variation

Color a yellowish shade and add dots to make an Asian pear. For an apple that's been cut, trace around the outside of the fruit in red.

Pineapple

Average

1 Draw a vertical oval.

Draw coming out to the sides

2 Above the oval, draw two diagonal lines.

3 Draw a zigzag to connect the lines and make the leaves.

4 Draw five lines of scalloping inside the oval.

Color in

Use scribbly lines to color in and create the look of the rough skin.

Variation

Use fan shapes to make the cut segments.

Cherries

Average

1 Draw a small circle.

2 Draw another circle the same beside it.

3 Connect the two circles with an upside-down V shape.

4 Draw a leaf at the top.

Color in

Color the fruit in red or pink.

Variation

Add eyes and mouths to make twin cherries.

Lemon

Easy

Leave open →

1 Draw a mountain shape and reflect the shape below it, leaving a gap in between.

2 Use small semicircles to connect the shapes.

3 Draw dots in the lower part.

Color in

Use bright yellow to make a fresh lemon.

Variation

To make a circular slice of lemon, draw a circle with two crosses overlapping in the middle. Draw drops of juice underneath... doesn't it look sour?

Strawberry

Easy

1 Draw a long, narrow stem.

2 Continue by drawing a scalloped line for the calyx.

From here

3 Draw an egg shape from both sides of the calyx.

4 Draw seeds inside.

Color in

Use green for the calyx and red for the fruit.

Variation

Try connecting two strawberries and adding the leaves and flower.

Banana

Average

1 Draw a long, narrow rectangle.

2 Draw one banana beneath the rectangle. Make it thicker toward the bottom.

Make the join narrower

3 Draw another banana next to it in the same way.

4 Add another one in the same way.

Color in

Add dense color in a cheerful yellow.

Variation

The shape of the skin is the key point when drawing a peeled banana.

Grapes

Difficult

1 Draw three circles in a row.

2 Add two circles underneath, then one circle underneath them.

Make a simple triangle

3 Draw a T shape at the top for the vine.

Color in

Use purple and reddish purple for a stylish effect.

Variation

Color the grapes green to make muscat grapes. It's fine to draw the grapes as lots of little circles too.

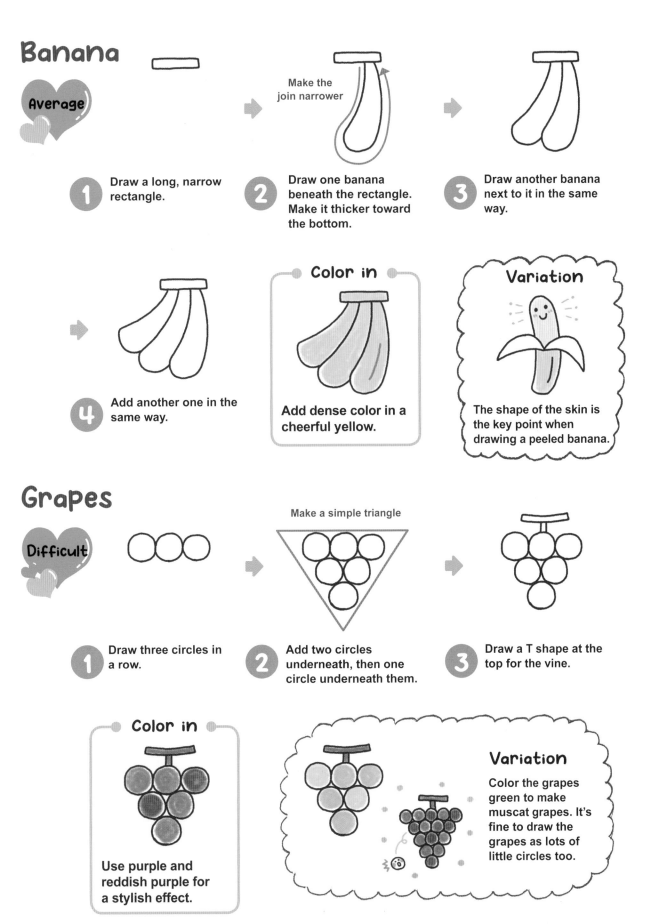

Tomato

Easy

1. Draw a star for the calyx.

2. Draw a circle coming from both sides of the calyx.

3. Draw a small circle inside the calyx.

Color in

Color in a strong red for a tasty look.

Variation

Use a heart shape for plum tomatoes. Draw eyes and a mouth and add curly lines to make them look like they are rolling around.

Eggplant

Average

1. Draw part of a square to make the stem.

2. Make this curved

   Draw a scalloped line connecting to the stem to make the calyx.

3. Draw an urn shape beneath the calyx.

4. Draw an upside-down exclamation mark at the bottom left for a shiny look.

Color in

Leave the shiny part white; don't color it in.

Variation

Add eyes, mouth and a bow to make a character.

Sugar Pea

Average

1 Draw part of a square to make the stem.

2 Draw a scalloped line connecting to the stem to make the calyx.

3 Draw a crescent moon shape beneath the calyx. Add curved lines inside.

Make slightly rounded

4 Draw a little circle at the edge of the crescent moon shape to add a pea. Draw eyes and a mouth.

Color in

Add triangles above the pea for expression.

Variation

Create a fun look by making the pea pop out.

Broccoli

Difficult

 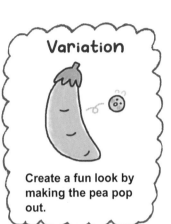

1 Draw a scalloped shape.

2 For the stem, draw a trapezium with a wide base underneath the scalloped shape.

3 Draw two lines next to the stem.

4 Draw an upside-down exclamation mark at the bottom left for a shiny look.

Color in

Use scribbly lines to color in to create a fluffy look.

Variation

Add eyes, mouth and bows for a stylish look.

Onion

Leave open

Average

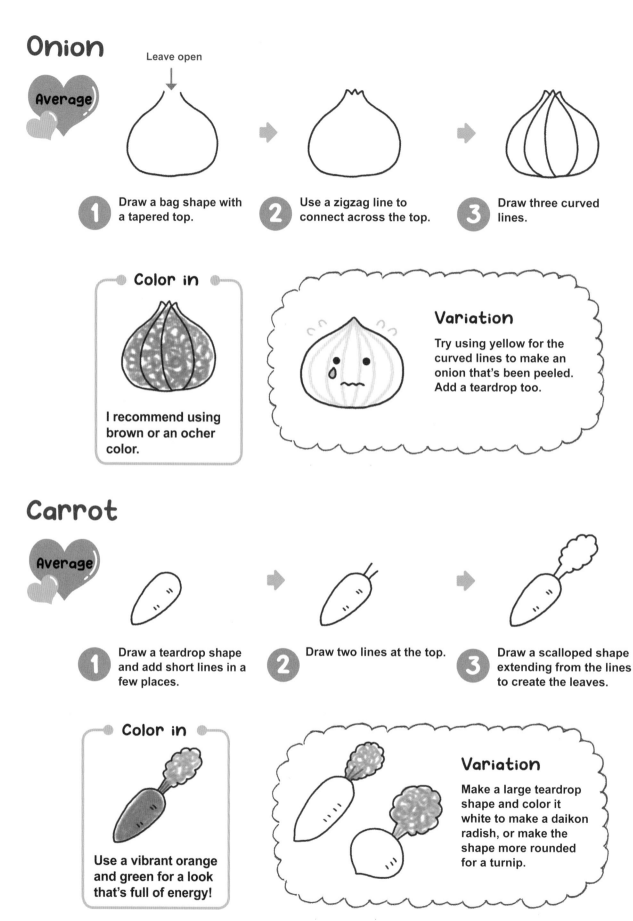

1 Draw a bag shape with a tapered top.

2 Use a zigzag line to connect across the top.

3 Draw three curved lines.

Color in

I recommend using brown or an ocher color.

Variation

Try using yellow for the curved lines to make an onion that's been peeled. Add a teardrop too.

Carrot

Average

1 Draw a teardrop shape and add short lines in a few places.

2 Draw two lines at the top.

3 Draw a scalloped shape extending from the lines to create the leaves.

Color in

Use a vibrant orange and green for a look that's full of energy!

Variation

Make a large teardrop shape and color it white to make a daikon radish, or make the shape more rounded for a turnip.

4 Kawaii Seasons & Holidays

Spring, summer, fall, winter! Halloween, Valentine's Day, Christmas! Give your seasonal and holiday favorites a cute Kawaii makeover.

Let's Draw Spring Illustrations

What makes you think of spring? Cherry blossoms, tulips, Easter eggs and candy from an Easter basket, all with a Kawaii spin.

Give heart-warming expression to tulips, dolls and Easter eggs for a true spring feeling.

Cherry Blossoms

Easy

Draw from here

1 Draw five dots to form a circle.

2 Starting from a dot, draw half a long heart shape.

3 Draw the other half connected to the first half.

4 Draw the remaining four shapes in the same way.

Color in

Color in a soft pink and scatter petals around the edge too.

Variation

Draw four hearts and add a stem to make a clover.

Tulip

Average

1 Draw a bowl shape, leaving it open at top.

2 Close off the shape by making a zigzag line to join each side.

Make the end pointy

3 Draw a vertical line beneath the flower and add a leaf at the end.

4 Draw another leaf on the other side.

Color in
Use whatever color you like and add eyes and a mouth.

Variation
Draw three in a row and place in a planter box.

Horsetail

Average

1 Draw an egg shape and add hash markings in the middle.

2 Add a long, narrow rectangle beneath the egg shape for the stem.

3 Make W shapes in a pattern down the stem.

4 Draw a smaller horsetail next to the first one.

Color in
Alternate two colors down the stem.

Variation
Draw the eyes and mouth to make an adorable spoon character.

Japanese Doll

Difficult

1. Draw a wide circle shape for the face.

2. Draw in the parted hair and color in. Add the eyes and mouth.

3. Draw a triangle for the kimono underneath the face.

Scalloped edges

4. Draw a fan inside the kimono and make a scalloped line for the crown on the head.

Color in

Use pink for the kimono and yellow for the crown.

Variation

Change the hairstyle and hat to make an emperor doll.

Easter Candy

Average

1. Draw a bow.

Make it large

2. Draw a circle extending from either side of the bow.

3. Draw a spiral in the center.

4. Draw a stick beneath the bow.

Color in

Diagonal stripes make for a stylish finish.

Key point

When drawing the spiral in step 3, start above the bow and work toward the center in a clockwise direction.

Easter Egg

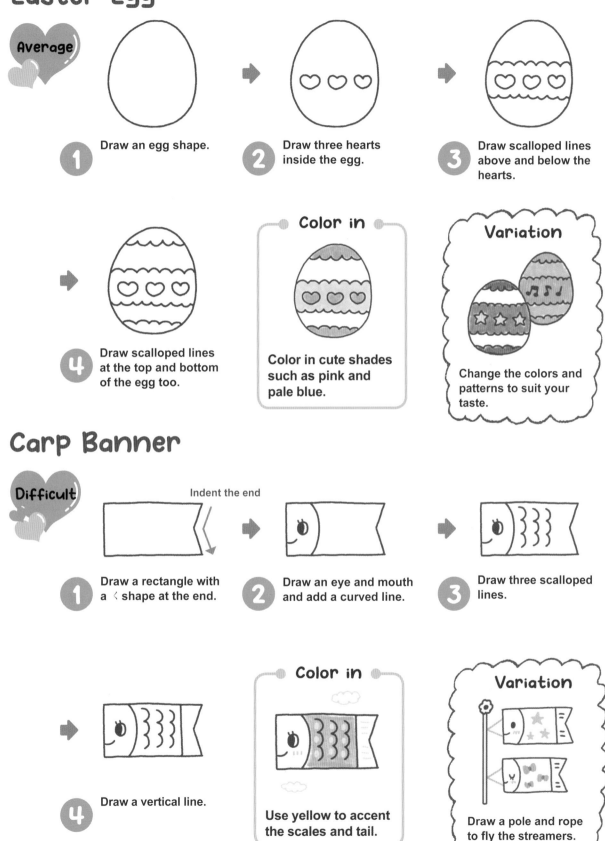

Average

1. Draw an egg shape.

2. Draw three hearts inside the egg.

3. Draw scalloped lines above and below the hearts.

4. Draw scalloped lines at the top and bottom of the egg too.

Color in

Color in cute shades such as pink and pale blue.

Variation

Change the colors and patterns to suit your taste.

Carp Banner

Difficult

Indent the end

1. Draw a rectangle with a 〈 shape at the end.

2. Draw an eye and mouth and add a curved line.

3. Draw three scalloped lines.

4. Draw a vertical line.

Color in

Use yellow to accent the scales and tail.

Variation

Draw a pole and rope to fly the streamers.

Let's Draw Summer Illustrations

Everyone loves summer vacation and the lazy pace of the season. I've gathered together motifs here that perfectly conjure images of summer.

The key point is to use cool colors that will burst through the summer heat.

Morning Glory

Average

○ ➡ ☆(in circle) ➡ (flower with leaves)

Make the middle leaf big

1 Draw a wide circle shape to make the flower.

2 Draw a large star in the middle.

3 At the lower left of the flower, draw a shape like three leaves joined together.

Color in

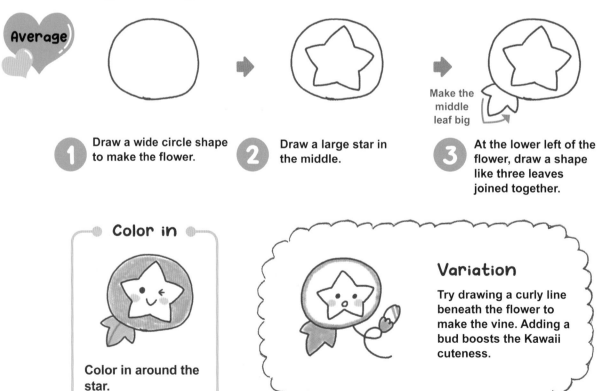

Color in around the star.

Variation

Try drawing a curly line beneath the flower to make the vine. Adding a bud boosts the Kawaii cuteness.

Sunflower

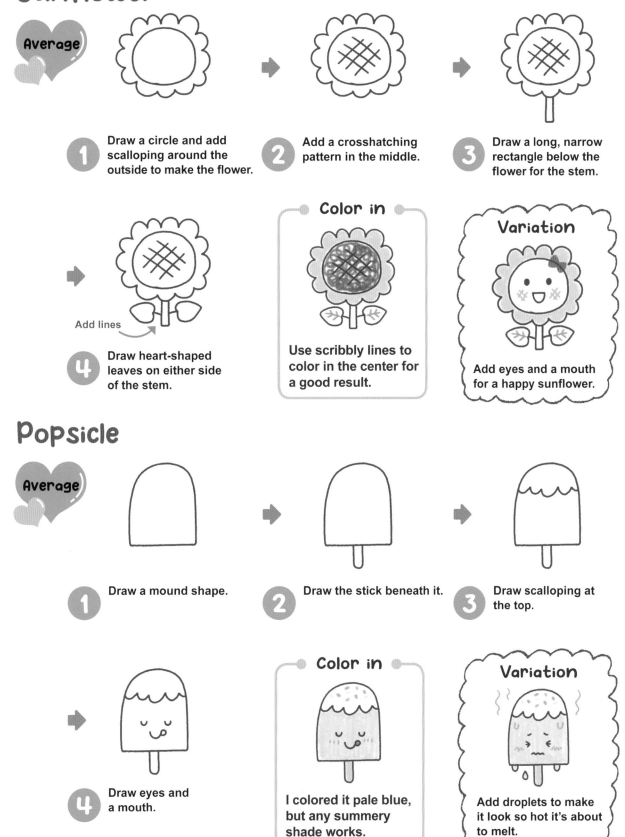

Average

1 Draw a circle and add scalloping around the outside to make the flower.

2 Add a crosshatching pattern in the middle.

3 Draw a long, narrow rectangle below the flower for the stem.

4 Draw heart-shaped leaves on either side of the stem.

Add lines

Color in
Use scribbly lines to color in the center for a good result.

Variation
Add eyes and a mouth for a happy sunflower.

Popsicle

Average

1 Draw a mound shape.

2 Draw the stick beneath it.

3 Draw scalloping at the top.

4 Draw eyes and a mouth.

Color in
I colored it pale blue, but any summery shade works.

Variation
Add droplets to make it look so hot it's about to melt.

Pool Ring

Easy

Don't draw inside the small circle

1. Draw a circle.

2. Draw a smaller circle inside.

3. Draw lines to create a cross.

4. Draw more lines in between.

Color in

Alternate red and white to color in.

Variation

Add a bow and scalloping to dress up the pool ring.

Goldfish in a Bag

Difficult

Make the ends slightly longer

1. Draw a scalloped line.

2. Draw an urn shape extending from both ends of the scalloped line.

3. Draw a horizontal line at the top.

4. Draw goldfish inside.

Color in

Trace a line of pale blue along the scalloping. Color the goldfish in red.

Variation

Draw the fish in a triangular bag for a summer festival vibe.

Fireworks

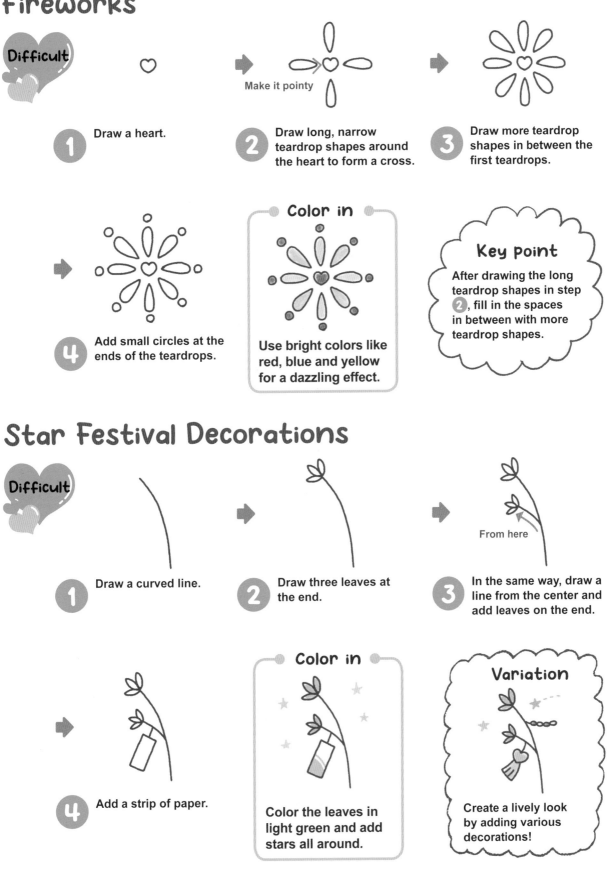

Difficult

1 Draw a heart.

Make it pointy

2 Draw long, narrow teardrop shapes around the heart to form a cross.

3 Draw more teardrop shapes in between the first teardrops.

4 Add small circles at the ends of the teardrops.

Color in
Use bright colors like red, blue and yellow for a dazzling effect.

Key point
After drawing the long teardrop shapes in step **2**, fill in the spaces in between with more teardrop shapes.

Star Festival Decorations

Difficult

1 Draw a curved line.

2 Draw three leaves at the end.

From here

3 In the same way, draw a line from the center and add leaves on the end.

4 Add a strip of paper.

Color in
Color the leaves in light green and add stars all around.

Variation
Create a lively look by adding various decorations!

Let's Draw Fall Illustrations

Crisp nights and spooky sights are the signs of the season. How fun is it to give your favorite Halloween characters a Kawaii-style upgrade?

Use colors such as orange, yellow and brown for an authentic fall look.

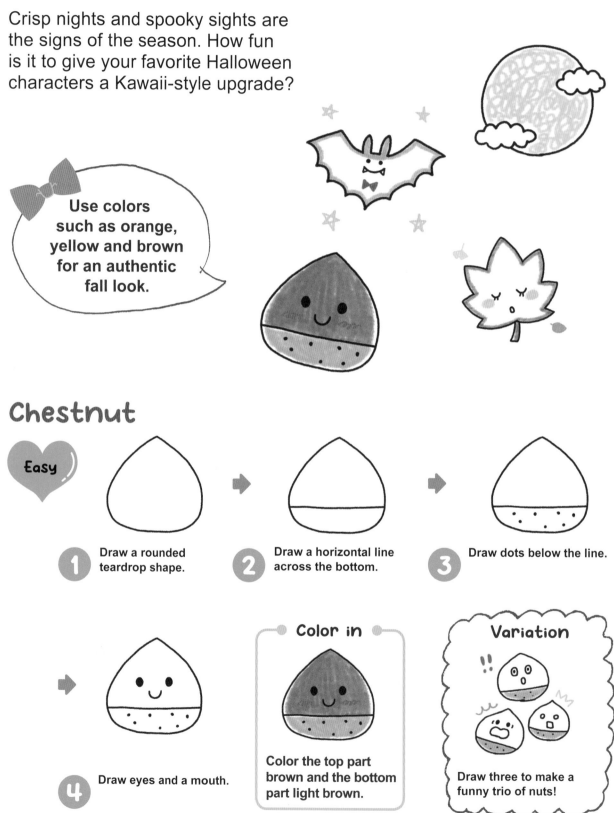

Chestnut

Easy

1 Draw a rounded teardrop shape.

2 Draw a horizontal line across the bottom.

3 Draw dots below the line.

4 Draw eyes and a mouth.

Color in

Color the top part brown and the bottom part light brown.

Variation

Draw three to make a funny trio of nuts!

Cosmos

Average

1 Draw a small circle.

Create a zigzag

2 Above the circle, draw a petal with a zigzag tip.

3 Add more petals in the same way to form a cross.

4 Add more petals in the gaps.

Color in

Color the petals pink and the center yellow.

Variation

Draw triangular wrapping with lots of flowers above it to make a bouquet.

Maple Leaf

Difficult

1 Draw part of a triangle.

2 Add similar shapes to either side.

3 Add smaller, tapered versions next.

Make a slight indentation

4 On either side, make small jagged lines and connect them in the center.

5 Draw the stem below.

Color in

Color in a reddish brown and add leaves around the outside.

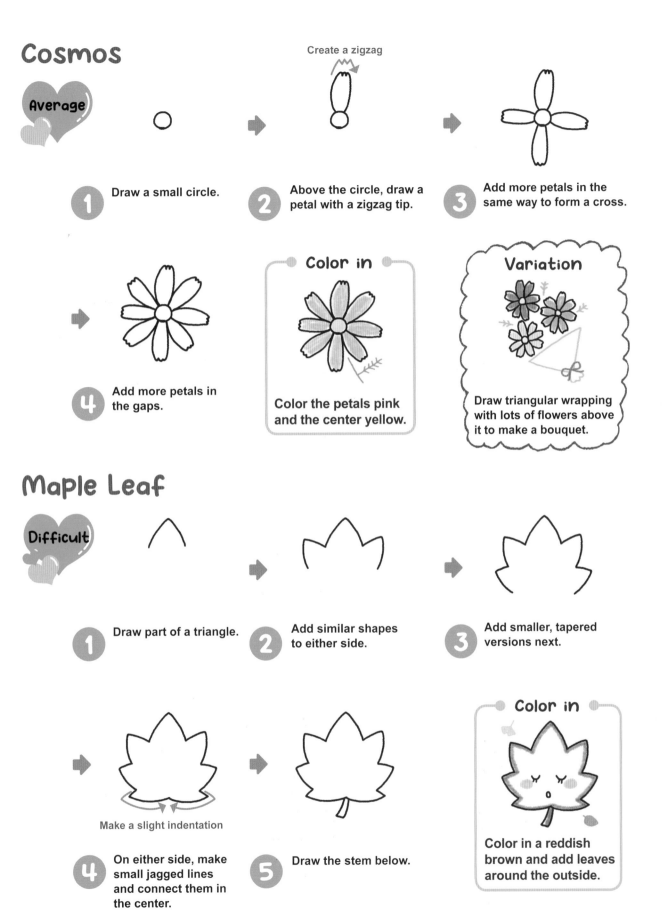

Harvest Moon

Easy

1. Draw scalloping to create a cloud.

2. Draw a cloud in the same way to the upper right.

Connect the clouds

3. Draw a semicircle to connect the clouds.

4. Draw another semicircle to connect the clouds on the other side.

Color in

Use scribbly lines to color in the moon in contrast to the clouds.

Variation

Draw a rabbit to create a scene with a rabbit on the moon.

Tower of Rice Cakes

Average

1. Draw a long, narrow rectangle.

2. Draw a square underneath with a circle inside; fill in the circle.

3. Draw three rice cakes in a row on top.

4. Draw two rice cakes above them, with another one on top.

Color in

Color in only the wooden container.

Variation

Add a vase with grass in it too!

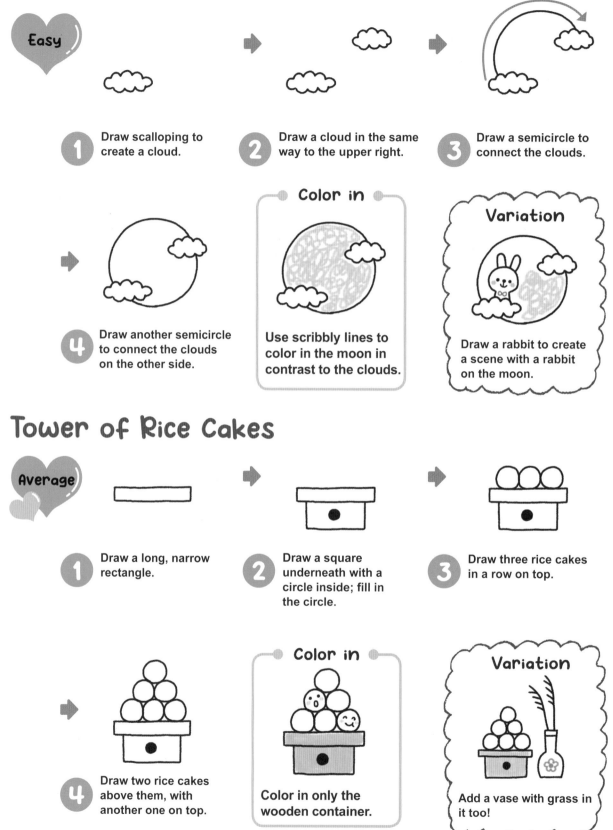

Jack O'Lantern

Average

1 Draw a curve above and one reflecting it below. Add a square on the top.

Start from here

2 Use a curved line to connect each end.

3 Do the same on the other side.

4 Draw triangles for eyes and zigzag lines to make the mouth.

Color in

Color inside the eyes and mouth in black.

Key point

When drawing the curves in step **1**, make the lower line shorter to create a neat shape.

Halloween Bat

Average

1 Draw rabbit-like ears.

2 Draw pointed mountain shapes on either side of the ears.

3 Draw a scalloped line in a V shape to connect the mountain shapes.

Make a V shape

4 Draw eyes and a mouth with triangular fangs on each side.

Color in

Trace the bat shape in gray.

Variation

Color in black and draw the moon and stars for a mysterious effect!

Let's Draw Winter Illustrations

Silly snowmen and dazzling Christmas decorations are just some of the winter wonders that make perfect Kawaii doodles.

Red and green are the common Christmas palette, but brighter baubles and highlights also appear!

Holly

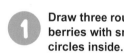

Make the outer edges pointy

1 Draw three round berries with small circles inside.

2 Make a scalloped line below the berries to draw one-half of the leaf.

3 Draw the other half and connect them, adding a line down the middle.

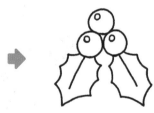

4 Draw the other leaf in the same way.

● Color in ●

Leave the little circles in the middle of the fruit white.

Variation

Add a bell underneath for a jingle bells motif. ♪

Christmas Wreath

Average

1. Draw a bow.

2. Draw a circle using a scalloped line from either side of the bow.

3. Make another scalloped circle inside.

4. Draw circles as decorations.

Color in

Use scribbly lines to create a leafy texture.

Variation

Add a bell for a gorgeous effect!

Christmas Tree

Difficult

1. Draw a star.

2. Draw scalloped lines starting from the star to create a triangle shape, open at the base.

Create a shape that gets broader toward the base

3. Draw a scalloped line to connect the edges.

4. Draw the trunk and add circles as decorations.

Color in

Use deep green for the leaves. Make the stars and decorations colorful.

Variation

Decorate with bows for an old-fashioned look.

Stocking

Average

1. Make a rectangle with a scalloped edge.

Make this side longer

2. Draw vertical lines from both ends of the scalloped rectangle.

3. Make a curve to connect the lines.

4. Add lines to the toe and heel and draw a bow. Add a loop at the upper right.

Color in

Leave the scalloping white.

Variation

Add presents peeking out at the top!

Snowman

Average

1. Draw a wide circle.

2. Draw a slightly bigger circle beneath the face.

3. Draw a trapezium on the top of the head and add in the eyes, nose and mouth.

4. Draw a row of buttons down the center of the body and add branches for arms on both sides.

Color in

I added a mitten at the end of one of the branches.

Variation

For the finishing touch, add a scarf!

Mochi Treat

Easy

1 Draw a rounded oval.

2 Draw a slightly larger rounded oval underneath.

3 Draw a little circle on top to make a tangerine.

Make it pointy

4 Draw dots inside the tangerine and add a leaf.

Color in

Color the tangerine orange. Adding a frilly line around the base of the mochi creates a cuter look.

Plum Flowers

Average

Connect the shapes

1 Draw a semicircle.

2 Draw semicircles on both sides.

3 Draw semicircles on both sides again to connect the shape.

4 Draw circles in each petal and add lines that all connect in the center.

Color in

Using a soft pink makes for a realistic look.

Variation

Add branches. For buds, draw circles with the letter y inside.

Popcorn

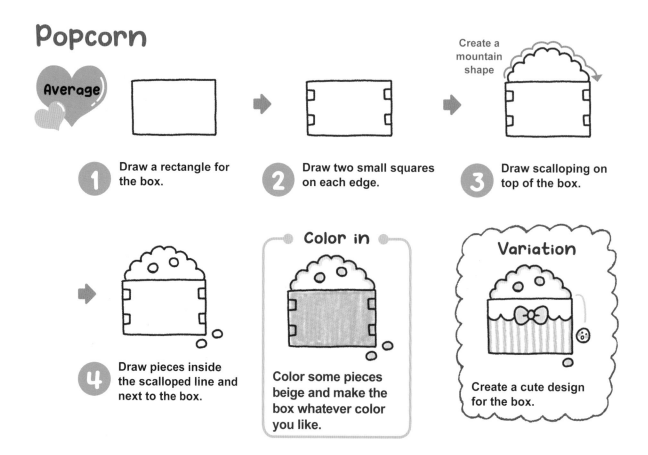

Average

Create a mountain shape

1. Draw a rectangle for the box.

2. Draw two small squares on each edge.

3. Draw scalloping on top of the box.

4. Draw pieces inside the scalloped line and next to the box.

Color in

Color some pieces beige and make the box whatever color you like.

Variation

Create a cute design for the box.

Valentine's Day Chocolate Box

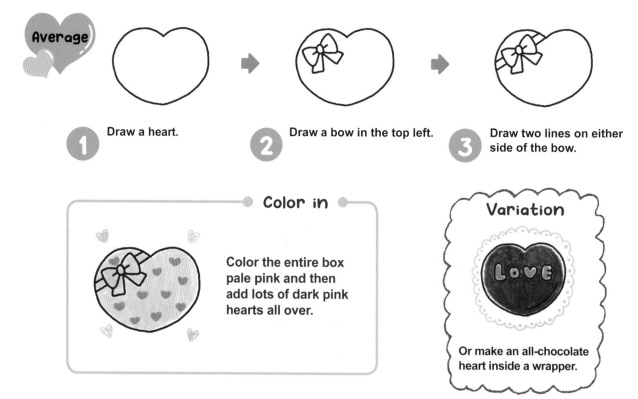

Average

1. Draw a heart.

2. Draw a bow in the top left.

3. Draw two lines on either side of the bow.

Color in

Color the entire box pale pink and then add lots of dark pink hearts all over.

Variation

Or make an all-chocolate heart inside a wrapper.

5 Give the Gift of Kawaii

Adding Kawaii-inspired illustrations to cards, presents and even little notes adds a personal touch and is sure to delight the recipient!

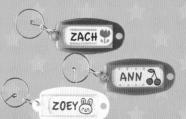

In this chapter, there are some projects that use scissors. Make sure you have an adult with you when you're using them.

For Your Family

Try adding illustrations of family members to cards for Mother's Day, Father's Day or invitations to family reunions or parties.

Mother's Day Card

I made a card like a bouquet by folding origami paper in thirds.

> ★ Materials

Origami paper, ribbon to decorate, colored pencils, craft glue

Flowers, sparkles
Draw various flowers for a gorgeous effect.
For how to draw, see ▶P124

Opened out

LOVE YOU!

Ribbon frame
Write a message in the middle.

Stick the ribbon on with glue.

Woman
Use your beloved mom as the model. If you draw your dad, you can make a Father's Day card too.
For how to draw, see ▶P12

Using small origami paper can be cute too.

How to draw a ribbon frame

Draw two curved lines. ➡ Draw a V shape at both ends. ➡ Add frilly lace.

Telephone Messages

I've made a handy magnetic telephone memo pad to stick to the fridge!

★ **Materials**

Drawing paper, magnet with sticker, pens, scissors

Stick on the magnet that has your icon on it to pass on your message.

Basic girl
For how to draw, see ▶P10

Dear Mom, I'd love to have pudding for my snack today. ♥ See you later!

Answer

You can have some once you've done your homework.
From Mom

Woman
For how to draw, see ▶P12

Write notes between family members, enclosing them in speech bubbles.

Write the date here

Try changing the shape of the speech bubble to match the content.
For how to draw, see ▶P127

It's handy to have magnets to suit the occasion.

How to attach magnets

stick on!

Cut drawing paper to the same size as the magnet and stick on.

Spoon and fork
Use this illustration to make meal requests.
For how to draw, see ▶P71

Man
For how to draw, see ▶P13

School
For how to draw, see ▶P125

Gifts for Friends

Kawaii doodles and decorations make snack time even more fun!

Lying flat

Wrapping for Shared Treats

Try adding illustrations to the wrapping for snacks and other shared treats.

Draw the illustration before tying the bag closed. Make the hair long and draw the face underneath.

Draw the eyes, nose and mouth to fill in the space.

★ Materials

Paper bag, ribbon, pens

Use a ruler when drawing stripes for an even result.

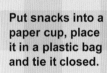

Put snacks into a paper cup, place it in a plastic bag and tie it closed.

★ Materials

Thin paper, pens

Flag
For how to draw, see ▶P125

★ Materials

Paper cup, plastic bag, wrapping paper, tie, pens

····· How to make a candy wrapper ·····

Decorate it with sweet and dessert-themed doodles.

Tie each end with a ribbon.

Christmas Cards

Cut a tree or wreath shape from paper and make it into a gorgeous card. It can be displayed standing up!

hearts, stars, bows, presents, candy canes
For how to draw, see ▶ P124, 125

Draw a line of dots and make circles with designs in them to hang below.

stocking
For how to draw, see ▶ P59

Santa's hat

★ Materials

Paper, pens, pencils

How to make a tree card

Fold paper in half and draw half a tree only, using pencil.
For how to draw, see ▶ P107

Keep folded and cut out the shape.

Cut out a large and small wreath with scalloped edges and layer them to stick together. Add a bow as decoration.

★ Materials

Paper, ribbon, pens, gluestick, craft glue, scissors

stars, snowflakes, bows
For how to draw, see ▶ P124, P125

Santa

How to draw Santa

Draw a triangle for a hat.

Draw a scalloped line to make a beard.

Draw the eyes and mouth inside the beard and draw a rectangle around them.

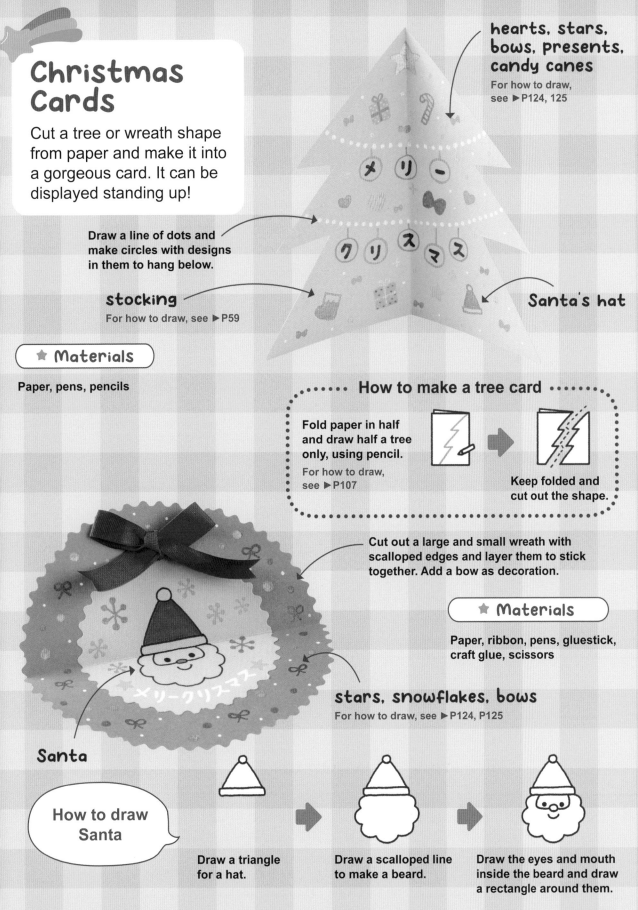

Birthday Present

There's nothing more special than receiving a gift wrapped in customized paper.

Draw colorful polka dots for a stylish look.

Basic girl
Draw a girl that looks like you.
For how to draw, see ▶P10

Draw the hands, then stick on masking tape and draw a bow.

JUST FOR YOU!

Happy Birthday

★ Materials

Paper cup, plastic bag, wrapping paper, tie, pens

Use a scalloped line to draw a heart.
For how to draw, see ▶P127

LOVE

Triangular Box for Valentine's Chocolates

Will you be my Valentine? What a perfectly Kawaii way to ask!

heart
Draw hearts with different patterns to make it pop!
For how to draw, see ▶P 124

★ Materials

Envelope, pens, scissors

How to make a triangular box

Cut off the top third of an envelope.

Collapse both sides in.

Fold over the top to close it.

Letter Set and Stickers

How about some original stationery, envelopes and stickers? It's fun to make the stickers, whatever shape you like.

cat pawprints
Making a border of pawprints is a great trick.
For how to draw, see ▶ P125

cat
For how to draw, see ▶ P29

Make a line of lace for a refined look.
For how to draw, see ▶ P126

cherries
For how to draw, see ▶ P87

★ Materials

Plain paper, envelopes, sheet of plain stickers, pens

I made some stickers like postage stamps.

snowflakes
For how to draw, see ▶ P124

bow
For how to draw, see ▶ P125

clover
For how to draw, see ▶ P94

soda
For how to draw, see ▶ P80

strawberry
For how to draw, see ▶ P88

umbrella
For how to draw, see ▶ P60

Draw outside the lines when coloring circular stickers to get a neat result when you remove them from the sheet.

dumpling
For how to draw, see ▶ P14

heart
For how to draw, see ▶ P124

★ Materials

Sticker sheet, pens, scissors

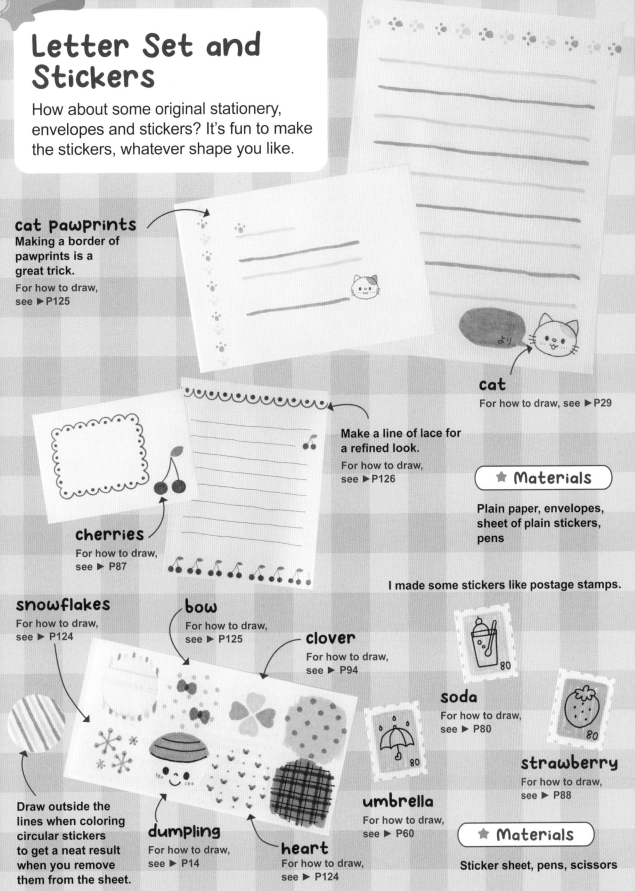

Gifts for Grandparents

Make your grandparents or relatives a handmade card to let them know you're thinking of them!

A Greeting or Birthday Card

Your grandparents or relatives will treasure these Kawaii-style keepsakes!

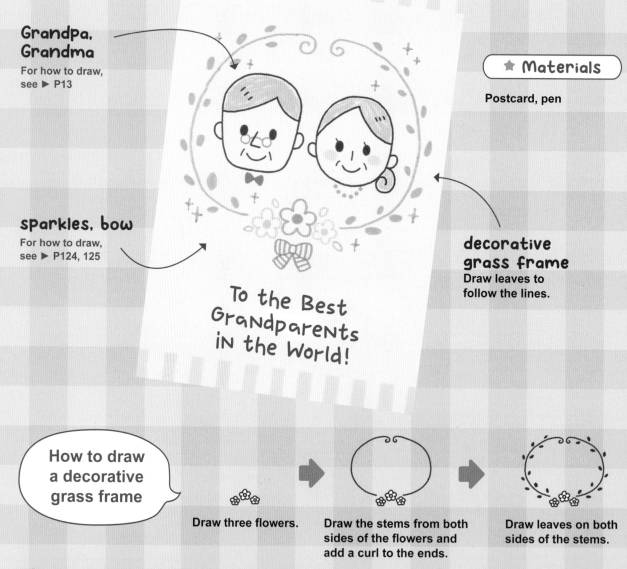

Grandpa, Grandma
For how to draw, see ▶ P13

sparkles, bow
For how to draw, see ▶ P124, 125

To the Best Grandparents in the World!

★ **Materials**

Postcard, pen

decorative grass frame
Draw leaves to follow the lines.

How to draw a decorative grass frame

Draw three flowers.

Draw the stems from both sides of the flowers and add a curl to the ends.

Draw leaves on both sides of the stems.

Photo Card

Draw on a photo of yourself to give as a gift. It makes a lively, fun card.

★ **Materials**

Photo, drawing paper, pen for writing on photos, gluestick

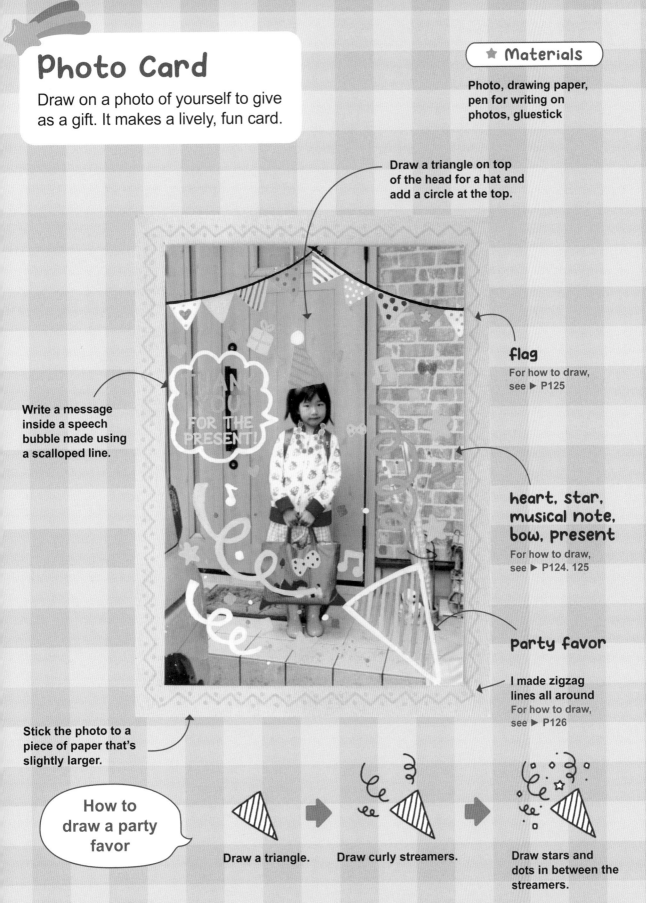

Draw a triangle on top of the head for a hat and add a circle at the top.

flag
For how to draw, see ▶ P125

Write a message inside a speech bubble made using a scalloped line.

heart, star, musical note, bow, present
For how to draw, see ▶ P124. 125

party favor

I made zigzag lines all around
For how to draw, see ▶ P126

Stick the photo to a piece of paper that's slightly larger.

How to draw a party favor

Draw a triangle.

Draw curly streamers.

Draw stars and dots in between the streamers.

For Everyone

Add illustrations to seasonal greetings to make postcards with a personal touch. It's good to change the design depending on the recipient, such as friends or teachers.

★ Materials

Postcard, pens

Midsummer Greetings

Use summer motifs such as the ocean or watermelons for that personal touch.

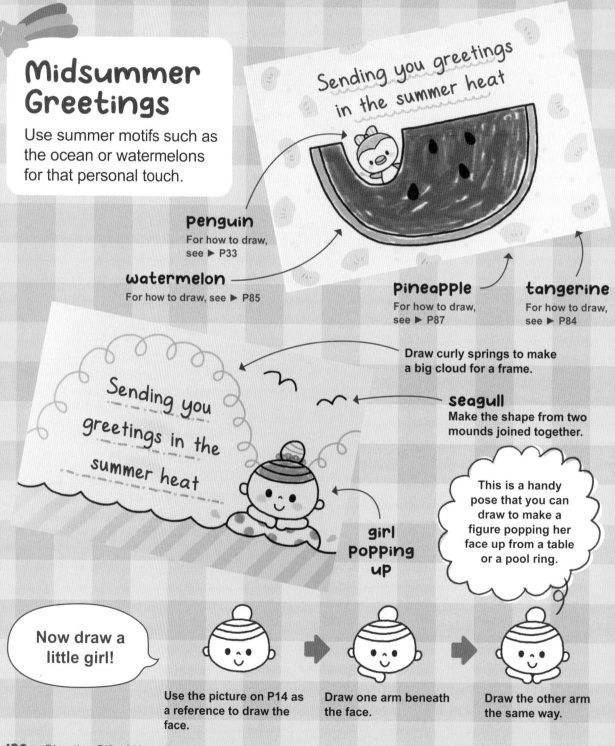

Sending you greetings in the summer heat

Penguin
For how to draw, see ▶ P33

watermelon
For how to draw, see ▶ P85

pineapple
For how to draw, see ▶ P87

tangerine
For how to draw, see ▶ P84

Draw curly springs to make a big cloud for a frame.

Sending you greetings in the summer heat

seagull
Make the shape from two mounds joined together.

This is a handy pose that you can draw to make a figure popping her face up from a table or a pool ring.

girl popping up

Now draw a little girl!

Use the picture on P14 as a reference to draw the face.

Draw one arm beneath the face.

Draw the other arm the same way.

Holiday Card

Use seasonal motifs to dress up your holiday greetings.

plum blossom
Draw a vertical line of plum blossoms in different sizes to decorate both edges.
For how to draw, see ▶ P109

HAPPY NEW YEAR

Little girl wearing a kimono

snowflake
For how to draw, see ▶ P124

snowman
Draw a snowman to fill the card and write inside his belly.
For how to draw, see ▶ P108

HAPPY NEW YEAR

★ **Materials**

Postcard, pen

How to draw a girl in a kimono

Refer to the illustration on p14 to draw the face.

Draw a triangle for the body and make a y for the collar and a horizontal line for the obi.

Draw a plum blossom in the hair for decoration.

Create Items for Yourself

Personalize the things around you in a fun way with Kawaii doodles! Your favorite illustrations will make every day a happy one. ♪

Stickers and Cards for Completing Tasks

Affix illustration stickers on a card when you've finished chores and homework.

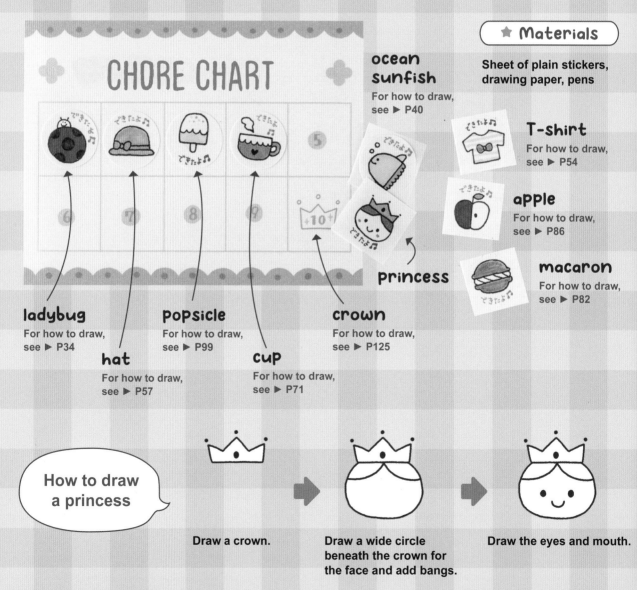

CHORE CHART

★ Materials

Sheet of plain stickers, drawing paper, pens

ocean sunfish
For how to draw, see ▶ P40

T-shirt
For how to draw, see ▶ P54

apple
For how to draw, see ▶ P86

macaron
For how to draw, see ▶ P82

princess

ladybug
For how to draw, see ▶ P34

hat
For how to draw, see ▶ P57

popsicle
For how to draw, see ▶ P99

cup
For how to draw, see ▶ P71

crown
For how to draw, see ▶ P125

How to draw a princess

Draw a crown.

Draw a wide circle beneath the crown for the face and add bangs.

Draw the eyes and mouth.

Name Tags

Add an illustration when attaching a name tag to personal belongings for a cute look!

★ Materials

Purchased name tags, pens

tulip
For how to draw, see ▶ P95

ZACH

cloud and sun
For how to draw, see ▶ P125

ZOEY

rabbit
For how to draw, see ▶ P28

ROB

cherries
For how to draw, see ▶ P87

ANN

Dust Jacket

How about your own original dust jacket to make reading fun?

Cut the cover to the size of the book and wrap it around.

donut
Add just one donut with a bite taken out for a unique look.

For how to draw, see ▶P82

Use black pen on brown paper for a stylish look.

nail polish
For how to draw, see ▶ P64

A line of bows is cute
For how to draw, see ▶ P 126

★ Materials

Paper the same size as the book, pens

Handy for all kinds of uses!
Let's Draw Icons and Decorations

Here, we look at easy-to-draw icons and decorations. Use the icons as accents or around letters of the alphabet. Frames and lines are super handy for decorating illustrations and lines of text.

Cute Icons That Are Easy to Draw

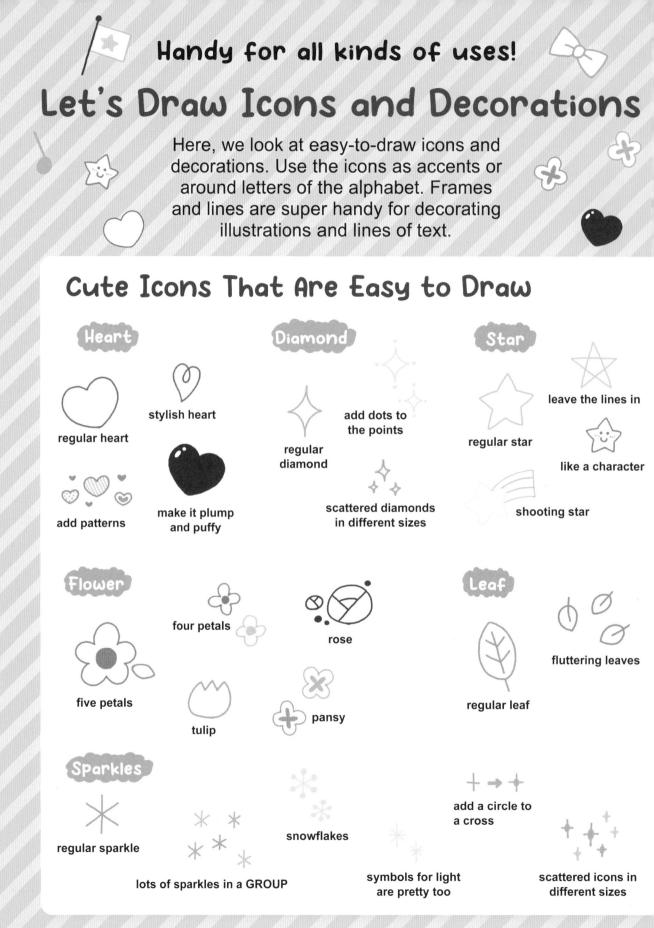

Heart

regular heart

stylish heart

add patterns

make it plump and puffy

Diamond

regular diamond

add dots to the points

scattered diamonds in different sizes

Star

regular star

leave the lines in

like a character

shooting star

Flower

four petals

rose

five petals

tulip

pansy

Leaf

regular leaf

fluttering leaves

Sparkles

regular sparkle

lots of sparkles in a GROUP

snowflakes

add a circle to a cross

symbols for light are pretty too

scattered icons in different sizes

Musical note

quarter note

eighth note

place them on a staff

Bow

regular bow

bow with the ends loose

cord tied in a bow

rounded bow

Crown

pointed crown

scalloped crown

School

high school

elementary school

Present

boxed present

present in a gift bag

Cane

regular cane

cane decorated with a bow

magic wand

Flag

regular flag

triangular flag

bunting

Footprints

cat pawprints

shoe prints

human footprints

tracks

Droplet

regular droplet

light rain

lots of droplets

Weather

sunny

cloudy

rain

downpour

snow

typhoon

thunder and lightning

rainbow

Let's Make Cute Lettering

Add the sun to morning greetings

Express feelings of gratitude with sparkles.

Scatter teardrops around the lettering.

Zigzag lines express shock.

Let's ★ Hang ★ Out

I added stars in between the letters and scribbly lines around the outside.

Draw each letter onto a heart. Use strong color for the letters.

Let's Draw Cute Lines

Adding circles inside scalloped lines creates a lace-like effect.

A lovely line created by connecting bows with dots.

Alternate stars with circles.

Add circles inside zigzag lines for an energetic effect.

Let's Draw Cute Frames

Draw a speech bubble with a scalloped line and add hearts around it.

Use a wavy line to make a sad speech bubble.

Use a thick pen to draw a square and add a polka dot pattern.

Draw hearts and add dots in between.

Use two pen colors and simply trace lines over and over.

I used different colors and sizes of circles to draw this.

A design that looks like it's held down with tape.

Draw leaves to decorate both sides of the stem and add flowers in the center at the bottom.

Draw a heart with a scalloped line and decorate with a bow at the bottom.

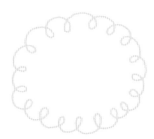

This is easy – simply draw a scribbly line!

A spiral notebook design. The pencil is the key point.

Use a zigzag line for messages that you want to stand out.

"Books to Span the East and West"

Tuttle Publishing was founded in 1832 in the small New England town of Rutland, Vermont [USA]. Our core values remain as strong today as they were then—to publish best-in-class books which bring people together one page at a time. In 1948, we established a publishing outpost in Japan—and Tuttle is now a leader in publishing English-language books about the arts, languages and cultures of Asia. The world has become a much smaller place today and Asia's economic and cultural influence has grown. Yet the need for meaningful dialogue and information about this diverse region has never been greater. Over the past seven decades, Tuttle has published thousands of books on subjects ranging from martial arts and paper crafts to language learning and literature—and our talented authors, illustrators, designers and photographers have won many prestigious awards. We welcome you to explore the wealth of information available on Asia at **www.tuttlepublishing.com**.

Published by Tuttle Publishing, an imprint of Periplus Editions (HK) Ltd.

www.tuttlepublishing.com

MANE SHITE KANTAN! ONNANOKO NO KAWAII ILLUST OEKAKI LESSON BOOK SHINBAN
© YUU, Nico Works. 2014, 2019.
English translation rights arranged with MATES Universal Contents Co. Ltd. through Japan UNI Agency Inc., Tokyo

English Translation ©2024 Periplus Editions (HK) Ltd.

ISBN: 978-4-8053-1781-5

Library of Congress Control Number: 2023944616

26 25 24 23   5 4 3 2 1
Printed in China   2310EP

TUTTLE PUBLISHING® is a registered trademark of Tuttle Publishing, a division of Periplus Editions (HK) Ltd.

Distributed by

North America, Latin America & Europe
Tuttle Publishing
364 Innovation Drive,
North Clarendon,
VT 05759-9436, USA
Tel: 1 (802) 773 8930
Fax: 1 (802) 773 6993
info@tuttlepublishing.com
www.tuttlepublishing.com

Japan
Tuttle Publishing
Yaekari Building 3rd Floor
5-4-12 Osaki
Shinagawa-ku
Tokyo 141-0032
Tel: (81) 3 5437-0171
Fax: (81) 3 5437-0755
sales@tuttle.co.jp
www.tuttle.co.jp

Asia Pacific
Berkeley Books Pte. Ltd.
3 Kallang Sector #04-01
Singapore 349278
Tel: (65) 67412178
Fax: (65) 67412179
inquiries@periplus.com.sg
www.tuttlepublishing.com